CREATING A
SenseSational
HOME

Books by Terry Willits

101 Quick Tips to Make Your Home Feel SenseSational

101 Quick Tips to Make Your Home Look SenseSational

101 Quick Tips to Make Your Home Smell SenseSational

101 Quick Tips to Make Your Home Sound SenseSational

101 Quick Tips to Make Your Home Taste SenseSational

Creating a SenseSational Home

For information about Terry Willits' speaking schedule or SenseSational® Home products, please send a self-addressed, stamped business envelope to:

SenseSational Homes, Inc.
P.O. Box 70353
Marietta, Georgia 30007
Telephone (770) 971-SENS
Fax (770) 971-0561

CREATING A
SenseSational
HOME

*Awaken the senses
to bring life & love to your home*

TERRY WILLITS

ZondervanPublishingHouse
Grand Rapids, Michigan

A Division of HarperCollinsPublishers

Creating a SenseSational Home
Copyright © 1996 by Terry Willits

Requests for information should be addressed to:

🏛 ZondervanPublishingHouse
Grand Rapids, Michigan 49530

Library of Congress Cataloging-in-Publication Data

Willits, Terry, 1959–
      Creating a senseSational home : awaken the senses to bring life and love to your home /
Terry Willits.
            p.   cm.
      ISBN: 0-310-20223-X (hardcover)
      1. Home economics.   2. Dwellings.   3. Interior decoration.   4. Christian life.   I. Title.
TX303.W564   1996
640—dc20   96-11706
                                                                                                                    CIP

This edition printed on acid-free paper and meets the American National Standards Institute
Z39.48 standard.

Edited by Rachel L. Boers
Interior Illustrations by Edsel Arnold
Interior design by Sherri L. Hoffman

Printed in the United States of America

98 99 00 01 02 /❖ QH/ 10 9 8 7 6 5

To my mother,
who has always filled her home
with life and love,
and to Bill,
the love of my life

CONTENTS

INTRODUCTION

I have been profoundly shaped by the home in which I was raised. We all are. A great deal of my love for my home today has been inspired by pleasant memories of the place I was nurtured in as a child.

When I was young we moved often, for my father was in the hospitality industry. No matter where we lived, home was a place I always looked forward to returning to because it was filled with satisfying sights, sounds, smells, tastes, and touches.

Far more than with just words, my mother taught me by example much of what I know and value about home. She exemplified diligence in every way and had many outside interests — but our home was a priority. My mother built our home with dignity, purpose, and joy. She understood that her investment into our home and lives had value. She passed on her positive attitude about the home to me.

As a little girl, my favorite pastime was to pretend my bedroom was my house. My sister and I would talk about our imaginary husbands, have pretend tea parties, and care for our dolls. At the age of five, I was already finicky about my bedroom being decorated tastefully. Little did I know that God was in the process of preparing me for my life calling.

Today I am an interior designer and married to my wonderful husband, Bill, who is an associate pastor at a church in Atlanta. As a designer, it is a great privilege to help clients transform their homes into places that bring them pleasure and peace of mind. As a pastor's wife, I am blessed to work with women of all ages and seasons of life, learning the different joys and challenges of their home lives. One thing I have learned about women: God has designed all of us with a desire to create a nest.

About eight years ago, Bill and I were teaching a class to a group of newly married couples. I casually mentioned my dream to someday (after we had and raised our family) pursue the passion of my heart: to encourage women to make their homes a pleasing place of ministry. After we spoke, I was surrounded by frustrated, yet eager women hungry to know what to do with their homes. The following day, I received a phone call from one of the young women asking me to consider speaking about the home at an upcoming women's retreat. It didn't take much prayer to realize God wanted me to pursue this passion now, not later.

As I prepared for the retreat, I was amazed and excited at how much God's Word had to say about the home. It confirmed what I already believed: the home is a very important place, not just to me, but to God.

As I combed many books available on the home, I found that most Christian books speak primarily on the *relational* ways to enhance our homes. Indeed, relationships affect the home atmosphere; but, the atmosphere we create in our homes can equally affect the relationships. On the flip side, I found that most secular books deal primarily with *physical* ways to beautify the home, leaving God, the ultimate Creator of all beauty, pleasure, and life out of the picture. And if he is not the builder, our efforts, no matter how noble, will be futile. The more I studied, the more I realized we need a balanced view on the homes we create.

As I have developed and refined my material over the years and shared it with many women in seminars, workshops, and retreats, I have been overwhelmed at the enthusiasm with which it has been received. Their response has shown me that home is a very important place to almost all women.

We all have dreams of the way we wish our lives and homes could be. After ten years of marriage, Bill and I still have an empty nest with no children. But God continues to show me that, even without children, my home and my life can bear rich fruit. So, with clear direction from a loving God and much encouragement from many enthusiastic women, I have compiled my material on the home into this book.

The ideas in this book are not necessarily profound, original, exhaustive, or even superspiritual, in and of themselves. They are to be used as a springboard to stimulate your own creativity. I am not suggesting you use all these tips in your daily life. Each of us has unique needs and desires for our particular home. I, myself, am in process, thinking of fresh ideas, finding new ways to do things. I don't use all of the ideas in the book all the time, but when I do use any of them, they make a difference in the atmosphere of my home.

As you read this book, choose just a few, simple ideas that appeal to you — things for which your home life is hungry. Then, store some of the others in the back of your mind for another time. It is my prayer that God will use this book as a tool to help inspire you to make your home all it can be.

So, put on some soft music, pour yourself an ice-cold glass of lemonade or a hot cup of tea, curl up in your favorite chair, and join me as we explore how to make our homes "SenseSational." Happy homemaking!

terry.

Chapter One

~

Making Sense
of It All

For by him all things were created ...
Colossians 1:16

MAKING SENSE OF IT ALL

More than any place on earth, I love my home. I love the way it smells after I've been away for a week. I love to sleep in my very own bed under my cozy comforter and sip tea from my favorite cup. I love to listen to my favorite music and the voices of those I cherish. I love to fill the kitchen shelves with my favorite foods. I love the colors that fill its rooms and the faces that fill my picture frames. I love to sit in my favorite spot and read my Bible and talk to God. And best of all, I love to share days, dreams, and hugs with my favorite people in all the world — my family.

Of course, our cheery, yellow house filled with familiarity hasn't always been my home. I, like you perhaps, have lived in many different places. Your current home could be a condominium, a cottage, or a castle. You may live alone or with a friend, a husband, or a family. Perhaps you are just beginning to build your nest and accumulate the things that make it a comfortable and pleasant home. Or you may be in the process of emptying your nest and simplifying your lifestyle. But no matter where you live or what your season of life, one thing is certain. From the day you were born, who you are and how you see the world has been greatly influenced by what takes place in the precious place called home. Most of us spend more time in our homes than any other spot on the globe. What we experience there marks us for life.

"Home is where you know your way in the dark."
— JoAnn Barwick

Our Refuge

Throughout Scripture, God is referred to as our spiritual refuge. We are told to run to him for safety, security, rest, replenishment, comfort, and never-ending love. In the same way, I believe God created our homes to be our physical refuge. He knew we would need a corner of the world to call our own. We go to our homes in hopes of finding physically many of the same qualities God offers us spiritually — a restful place, safe from the storms and stresses of the

world, filled with love, comfort, and absolute acceptance. A warm bed, an encouraging word, a tasty meal, a crackling fire all give comfort, security, and love. Home is to be the refuge we run to after doing battle in the world. It should be where we are reminded of who we are, to whom we belong, and what really matters in life. Home needs to be a safe place where we house not only our bodies, but our hearts and our souls.

A Woman's Touch

I am glad God made me a woman. Society today seems to be moving back toward acknowledging the vast differences between men and women. God has a unique and specific purpose for everything he creates. Genesis 2:18 explains at least part of God's reason for the creation of woman: "It is not good for the man to be alone. I will make a helper suitable for him." He made woman to complement man, to enhance and fulfill him in areas that he lacks. He gave women qualities that are different from men, but equally important to life.

Though we each express it differently, most every woman has a desire to gather, nest, and nurture. Some more than others, perhaps. How we perceive and meet these desires will be influenced by our training, modeling, life experiences, and values. But for the most part, God purposely created in women this gathering, nesting, nurturing desire to help make the world a more beautiful and secure place. It can also bring to us, as well as to those whose lives we touch, great pleasure and fulfillment.

"Our responsibility has not changed. We, as women, are responsible for our nests."
— Jeannie Hendricks

Proverbs 14:1 speaks true to women even today: "The wise woman builds her house . . ." This Scripture does not suggest that we physically build the structure of our homes; but it does imply that we are to be a source of strength and an example of diligence for our families. If we are wise, we will care for our household and pay attention to its details so that it will not only remain intact, but stand firm. Opportunities are all around us: noticing when someone needs to be held without a word, filling the kitchen with the fragrance of a favorite meal, decorating the rooms in a comfortable and inviting way, cleaning out the refrigerator and loading it with delicious food, dropping a love note in a lunch bag, turning off the television to listen to a heartache, lighting a candle to quiet minds after a hectic day.

The wise woman who builds her house is attuned to the little details her home needs at that particular moment.

As women, our homes are possibly our greatest sphere of influence in this world. God designed us to be thermostats for our environment, especially our homes. A thermostat is different than a thermometer. A thermometer simply measures the temperature of its surroundings; a thermostat, however, sets and regulates the temperature of its surrounding. It *determines* the temperature, hot or cold, comfortable or miserable.

You may not be able to control all of the sights, sounds, smells, tastes, and touches you or your family encounter outside your home, but you *can* have tremendous influence over the atmosphere inside your home by how you stimulate the senses. The color paint you choose, the tone and volume of your voice, the fragrance of the room, the table you set for dinner, the firmness of your mattress, the food with which you fill your pantry — all of these are simple choices you can make to influence your home in a positive way.

As women, we have an incredible ability to affect our surroundings in a powerful way. The more aware we are of our influence, the more motivated we will be to exercise that influence by making our homes a pleasant place. As we do, lives will be blessed.

"She watches over the affairs of her household . . ."
— Proverbs 31:27

OUR SENSES

God has made us sensual beings. In his goodness and creativity, he has given us eyes to see, ears to hear, noses to smell, mouths to taste and talk, and bodies to feel. Each sense is a rich blessing that enhances our life in a unique way and can bring immense pleasure or pain. Though every sense is wonderful, we seldom encounter only one at a time. Instead, God has intricately wired them together to allow us to experience all dimensions of life as we take in the world around us.

What if God had created the world to be only one color, say beige? What if he had created only one, tasteless food for us to eat? What if the whole world was like many products today, unscented?

What if the entire earth was absolutely silent? No noise, anywhere. What if we could not feel hot or cold, sharp or smooth, pleasure or pain? Life would be not only predictable, it would be dull.

Most of us have been graciously given five wonderful and unique senses. I wonder, if we experienced even a temporary loss of any one of these senses, would we have a renewed thankfulness for the way God has blessed us? By awakening the senses in our homes, our worlds will also be greatly enhanced.

"Your home should . . . be a greenhouse where you . . . flourish to your full potential."
— Vicki Kraft

Our Senses Bring Life

Our stimulated senses are the way we experience life. They inform us, warn us, welcome us, nourish us, encourage us, soothe us, stimulate us, and most of all, satisfy us. As we awaken the senses in our home, we bring life to it. While a dark, silent, musty home is far from pleasing, the soft light of a lamp, a flickering candle, soothing music, or a wonderful smell brings enjoyment and energy.

Just as God has created women to be the ones to bring life into this world, so he has entrusted us with the primary privilege of bringing life into our homes. If something is alive, it is vibrant and growing and changing. We too need to be vibrant, growing, and changing in order to continue to view our homes in fresh ways. If we do, our home atmosphere will be exciting and enjoyable. If we are bored with our homes and our lives, we are not taking advantage of all God has intended for us.

I have never understood those who insist on eating the same food for dinner every night, like beef and potatoes. What a joy in life they are missing out on by refusing to tantalize their taste buds with the many different and delightful foods that God has created! I love what one of my husband, Bill's, seminary professors said, "God is not boring. People are boring!" Life becomes dull when we make it dull. To fill our homes with life, we need to continually stimulate our senses in ways that are pleasing to ourselves and honoring to God.

When we awaken our senses to all of the blessings of life, opportunities abound to make home an exciting place. Rearrange your furniture. Move your accessories. Try a new recipe. Dust off a favorite album and fill your home with its music and memories. Overflow a pitcher with fragrant flowers or add a few fluffy pillows to your sofa. You hold the keys to bringing life to your home.

Our Senses Express Love

Stimulating the senses not only allows life to bloom, it also communicates love. When you love someone, you naturally want to do things for them that will bring them pleasure. Preparing a favorite meal, or surprising someone with a fresh bouquet of fragrant flowers, are ways we express love from one person to another. Similarly, God loves us so much that he has given us thousands of flavors to enjoy, and gardens of colorful, scented flowers to bring us pleasure. As we satisfy the senses in our homes, we reflect the love and care of our Heavenly Father.

Do you have fond memories of visits to someone's home where you were showered with love? How did your host or hostess stimulate your senses to make your time there extra special? Don't underestimate the small acts of love you do in your home. Though those extra touches take little effort on your part, they may leave a lasting impression in someone's heart.

And don't forget yourself! The little acts of kindness we do for ourselves express love as well. Sipping a steaming cup of tea or soaking in a warm bath can replenish us so that we, in turn, can shower others with love. We are God's vessels for pouring out his love, but if we are empty we will have nothing to offer others.

"What we learn with pleasure, we never forget."
— Alfred Mercier

Our Senses Make Memories

Stimulating the senses in a positive way in our homes can bring immense, immediate satisfaction. Warm hugs and warm meals both bring pleasure. But perhaps the biggest blessing of celebrating the senses in our homes is what they do over time. When a sense is stimulated frequently in a particularly pleasant or unpleasant way, it becomes locked in our brains as a memory to be recalled over and over again. Later, when that same smell or sound reoccurs, we are not only instantly reminded of an earlier time and place, we are also filled with the emotions of that previous experience.

The role of the senses in memory is so strong that many memories in life are often simply recollections of our stimulated senses.

Ask someone to describe a favorite memory of his past and no doubt it will conjure up a myriad of satisfying sights, smells, sounds, tastes, and touches. A love song on the radio may stir up emotions from a relationship long past. The smell of a rose may instantly evoke memories of visits to a favorite aunt's home. The faces in a picture frame may remind you of shared times with family and friends.

The more senses involved in any experience, the more we will retain its memory. Think about Christmas. Indeed, Christmas is a special and sacred time to focus on the birth of Jesus Christ; but what makes the Christmas season overflow with sentimental memories is how our senses are stimulated throughout the holidays — Christmas music playing on the stereo, bells jingling, the fragrance of a freshly cut pine tree adorned with twinkling lights and treasured ornaments that have been collected over the years, the smell and sound of a crackling fire, the taste of Christmas goodies. All these sensations keep Christmas alive in our memories.

Pleasant memories can multiply life's joys. By awakening all of the senses in our homes, we can not only enjoy the blessings they bring to us today, we can use them to bring back special memories to reflect upon and relish for years to come.

Our Senses Make Harmony

Creating a "SenseSational" home is much like conducting an orchestra. Though the conductor may have a special love for one instrument in particular, it is not necessary that he or she be an accomplished, master musician on all of the instruments. Instead, it is enough to have an understanding of each instrument and the awareness of how it enhances the total, pleasing sound. In the same way, you may not cook like Julia Child or decorate like Laura Ashley, but you can still create a beautiful, balanced melody by learning enough about each sense to make it a part of your home's harmony.

We all have gifts and talents, likes and dislikes. I love to decorate and make my home visually appealing; it comes naturally and brings me great pleasure. However, I would not be providing a balanced environment in my home if that was all that was important to me. So, although it takes more effort for me to be motivated to fill my home with delicious food and prepare healthy meals, I do it

"When a house speaks, you can walk in and see and hear, smell and touch, the echoes of many lives . . ."
— Charlotte Moss

because I have learned its importance and value to my home. Seeing the joy my extra effort brings to loved ones is well worth stretching myself beyond my natural tendencies.

What is the sense you most enjoy stimulating in your home? Which seems most neglected? Maybe you are so busy decorating your home that you have failed to take time to lend a listening ear or offer a tender touch to a loved one. Perhaps you are especially organized, but have no idea how to make your home look warm and welcoming. Life is a continual balancing act. Evaluate where your home life is on the scale of senses and ask God to help you balance it by stretching you in new areas. You may need to listen to a few pointers from someone else, take a course, or seek assistance in an area of homemaking in which you do not feel confident.

Our Senses Attract

When stimulated, our senses can have a powerful influence over our behavior. Because of this, appealing to our senses can make our homes alluring and attractive. Perhaps we could learn a lesson on the powerful influence of the senses from an expert, the wayward woman in Proverbs 7. This woman had learned from experience that the way to entice a man into her home was to stimulate all of his senses.

First, "She took hold of him and kissed him . . . (verse 13)." Obviously, this woman knew well the power of physical touch in making someone feel important. She came upon the man by surprise and touched him.

"No amount of money could buy the feeling that swept over me — the noise and pace of the world were strangely muffled by the sounds and smells of home."
— Chuck Swindoll

Then she tempted his taste buds. "I have fellowship offerings at home; today I fulfilled my vows (verse 14)." This wayward woman had some delicious meat left over from the sacrifice she had offered on the altar that day and was going to use it to seduce him.

Next, she flattered the man. Verse 15 says, "So I came out to meet you; I looked for you and have found you!" In other words, she tickled his ears with her smooth talk. All of us want to be noticed, sought out, and made to feel special and important. By telling the man words he wanted to hear, she enticed him.

The woman subtly moved the conversation to the tempting trap, her bedroom. She got him to visualize her bed in verse 16: "I have covered my bed with colored linens from Egypt." Her bed was beautiful to behold — covered with layers of brilliant, expensive fabrics.

Finally, the woman lured the man by appealing to the all-powerful sense of smell. In verse 17, she tempts his nose, saying, "I have perfumed my bed with myrrh, aloes and cinnamon." Who isn't attracted by something that smells wonderful? Then, "All at once he followed her like an ox going to the slaughter (verse 22)." The young man yielded to her, unable to resist her any longer. Why? He was in the company of a woman who knew the incredible power of the senses.

I am not trying to glorify this woman's actions or justify those of the young man. But these verses clearly demonstrate the tremendous influence our senses can have on our behavior.

Are you frustrated by a husband or children or even friends who never seem to hang around home for long? Think about your home. Is it alluring and desirable? If your family's needs for love, pleasure, and security are not being satisfied in your home, they are much more likely to be tempted to find it somewhere else, somewhere that God never intended. It makes sense to enjoy the wonderful senses God has given us by stimulating those senses in our homes. They are powerful indeed!

"Home is where life makes up its mind."
— Hazen Werner

THE BIG PICTURE

Creating a "SenseSational" home is not meant to be an end in itself. It is, however, the *means* to an end, because the atmosphere we create in our home directly affects our home's most important aspect: the relationships we have there. We want our home to have an atmosphere that allows souls to be replenished, love to flourish, and God to be glorified. Sights, sounds, smells, tastes, and touches are merely a means to minister to our loved ones while here on earth. Furnishings and fabrics will someday be gone. Food will be eaten. Music and laughter will be hushed. Fragrance will no longer fill the rooms. But the memories of the atmosphere and the relationships in our home will live on forever.

I believe the primary reason God has blessed us with our wonderful senses is so that we would stand in awe of him and be grateful for his goodness to us. Did God create the vast oceans just so that we could enjoy the soothing sights and sound of waves crashing or the tasty pleasure of salt water on our lips? Certainly, he created the oceans in part for these purposes, but most of all, I believe he made the wide waters of this world so we would be amazed by his mighty power and creativity.

The ability to enjoy life is one of God's richest blessings to us. It is easy to feel an overwhelming sense of God's presence and power at the beach, but it is much more difficult to experience and be grateful for his involvement in the more ordinary and mundane experiences of my home life — like the peaceful sound of a dryer as it heats the laundry, or the softness and warmth of the fabrics to my hands as I touch and fold them. God wants us to know that he is just as involved in these simple experiences of our home life as he is in the vast oceans. He wants us to enjoy them and be grateful to him for them as well. The extent to which we enjoy our home life greatly influences how we enjoy the world. There is no greater way to fill our homes and hearts with life and love than by awakening our wonderful, God-given senses.

"Ears that hear and eyes that see — the LORD has made them both."
— Proverbs 20:12

Tiny Thought

Lord,
Each sense that I have
Is a blessing from above.
May I celebrate your goodness
As I fill my home with love.

Chapter Two

—❧—

Pleasing the Eye

He has made everything beautiful in its time . . .
Ecclesiastes 3:11

A Glimpse of Sight

It's hard to look at a beautiful painting without it revealing something about the artist: his or her passions, personality, and priorities. So it is with God. When we look at all that he has made — the breathtaking sunrises and sunsets, the rolling mountains, the beautiful oceans, sandy shores, and bouquets of flowers in all colors, sizes, and shapes — we get a giant glimpse of the master of creativity. God is the ultimate Creator of all beauty, pleasure, and order. He is the artist of the universe, and he created us in his image. He has also provided us with the ability to create beauty and has given us the sensitivity to appreciate it. Is it any wonder that we desire to create beauty in our own personal worlds, our homes?

Our eyes are the most significant sense organs we have for appraising and understanding the world around us. They are our windows to God's world; what we take in with them provides many of the temporary pleasures of life on earth. Not only do our eyes help us carry on almost every activity of our daily life, they help us interpret life through what we see with them. And because most of us spend more time in our homes than anywhere else in the world, making them visually appealing can greatly affect our outlook on life.

The sense of sight is undeniably important to God. He allocated two-thirds of the minds' conscious attention and two-thirds of the information stored in the brain to what our eyes view. The eyes are the only sense organs that can, without assistance, overcome great distances. Looking down from an airplane window, we are able to observe a huge span of earth hundreds of miles below. Gazing up at the sky at night, we can view spectacular stars trillions of miles away. In fact, because we can take in so much of the world by what we see with our eyes, it is easy to get distracted and fail to focus on the magnificent beauty right before us. When was the last time you looked in awe at the simple beauty of a single flower? The gentle flicker of a flaming candle? The vivid blue of a clear sky? The tender eyes of one you love? All these beautiful glimpses are gifts from God as well.

Earth is crammed with heaven.

Beauty Attracts

There's no getting around it, beauty attracts. When you see something beautiful, it catches your eye, often captivates you for a moment and may even capture you and draw you in. Think of a pretty dress hanging in a store window. You first glance at it through the corner of your eye as you walk past the storefront. Then you stop and gaze at it to see if it is truly as beautiful as it appears. Now you notice it is not only lovely, but it is in your favorite color and style, so you walk into the store to study the dress and the price tag. It's your size, and the price is right. Before you know it, you're in the dressing room trying it on, all because it pleased your eye and attracted you.

Making our homes beautiful can create a similar response. When your home is visually appealing to you and your family, when it is a right "fit" for your personal style, it pleases you and draws you into its surroundings. There is no other place in the world you would rather be, and you and your loved ones will do everything possible to get there. By contrast, many people whose homes are in a constant state of disarray and disaster *avoid* going home! Don't underestimate the attraction of beauty in your home.

Beauty Communicates

If someone walked into and around your home while you were not there, what would they learn about you? Whether we want to admit it or not, how our home looks communicates our personalities, passions, and priorities. Our home tells our life stories: who we are, who we love, where we've been, what we do, and what we like.

When I look at the beauty God created in nature, the way he wondrously crafted the details of the world, I am overwhelmed with his love for me. I am amazed that he would care enough to create such beautiful things in life to enjoy. In the same manner, by making my home orderly and attractive, I communicate *my* love and care to those who live under my roof.

It takes time, effort, energy, and money to make a home look pleasant. In her book, *The Hidden Art of Homemaking*, Edith Schaeffer confirms the importance of a creating a pleasant home atmosphere: " . . . for the Christian who is consciously in communication with the

"Innovation comes in the little details that — like happy surprises — pop up to delight the eye . . ."
— Tonin MacCallum

Creator, surely his home should reflect something of the artistry, the beauty and order of the One whom he is representing, and in whose image he has been made."

As an interior designer, I have found that although most women love their homes and want them to look pleasant, they feel inadequate when it comes to making them that way. I hope the pages that follow will help you begin to gain confidence by showing you a few ways you can begin to make your home beautiful. Start simply. The smallest touches that please the eye can communicate the greatest love. Is there one area of your home that is an eyesore or unpleasant distraction? If so, that's where you need to begin to bring beauty to your home.

"The eye is the lamp
of the body."
— Matthew 6:22

Beauty Energizes

What is it about a beautiful, sunny day that inspires you to open the windows, put on some upbeat music, and celebrate life? Why does a gloomy, cloudy day make you want to curl up with a good book or take a nap? And why is it that a "bad hair" day makes you feel rotten all over, while treating yourself to a new haircut seems to energize you? The difference is beauty. God, in his goodness, created in women a desire to be surrounded by beauty.

Studies have been done that prove that our bodies' biological functions are actually enhanced in the presence of nature's beauty. Our blood pressure goes down, our heart rate lowers, and stress hormones drop. And as our bodies celebrate the beauty around them, they are replenished and energized. These same studies verified that patients who have undergone surgery or serious illness recovered faster in a hospital room that had a view of trees than those in rooms overlooking a concrete wall.

Our efforts to make a visually appealing home need not be in vain if they can enhance our health and outlook on life. When we create an atmosphere that is pleasing to our eyes and beautiful in our sight, we are replenished by being there. As we are replenished, we are energized to enjoy life and all it holds.

Beauty Today

Society today has fallen into the beauty trap. Our world worships beauty — beautiful people, beautiful fabrics, beautiful furniture, beautiful homes. By stressing the visual appeal of our homes so disproportionately to other equally important qualities, our culture communicates that beauty is all that matters. Beauty has become more than a goal; for many, it has become a god. But in striving solely for material beauty, we are simply building monuments to ourselves. When we leave God out of the equation, we worship that which is beautiful, rather than worshiping the provider of beauty, God himself.

With an imbalanced emphasis on the visual appeal of the home, many women today feel extremely insecure. Why? Because their homes don't look like what the magazines portray they should look like. What today's society forgets to tell us is that pleasing the eye alone can be dreadfully deceiving. I have been in many beautifully decorated homes where sadness fills the walls. I have also been in many modestly decorated homes that radiate warmth, comfort, love, and life.

Two other views on beauty neglect its place in the home altogether. One view springs from an attitude of ungratefulness. People simply don't take care of that with which God has entrusted them. The other mind-set is one of false spirituality. It suggests that one is somehow more spiritual if one neglects the visual appeal of the home. I, however, believe God would have us use the resources he has given us to create a pleasant place where lives can be blessed and he can be glorified. Our love for and appreciation of the beauty that God has given us needs to be addressed in a balanced fashion as an important ingredient in our homes.

"Our goal for our homes should not be designer-showhouse perfection but a place with memories, successes and endearing flaws."
— JoAnn Barwick

BEAUTIFUL EXTERIORS

Have you ever taken a leisurely drive through a neighborhood and come across a house that particularly appealed to you? What made it so pleasing? Have you ever stepped up to the front door of a home for the first time and been immediately fascinated by its charm? Like a personal introduction, your home's exterior should extend a warm welcome to friends and family alike, giving them a glimpse of what is yet to come.

When we lived in Dallas, there was a charming home that I would go out of my way to drive past. It was a rather small house on a somewhat busy street, but it was a house that was obviously overflowing with love and care. Just driving past it made me smile. I often fought the urge to go up to the front door and knock, just so I could meet the owners and solve my curiosity about what kind of people would live there. I knew they must be warm and friendly; their home's exterior said so. The sidewalks were lined with a rainbow of colorful flowers. There was a huge American flag blowing in the breeze. The front porch held a few wicker rockers and an old armoire that seemed to say, "Come on in, you're home!" A silly, painted wooden cow grazing in the green grass told me that the owners had a sense of humor. What does your home's exterior say about you? Making our entrances pleasing to the eye may bless more people than we think.

The light that shines the farthest shines the brightest near home.

The Friendly Front Door

When we set out to make our homes beautiful, all too often it seems we forget about the front door. Perhaps, if you have a back door, you seldom see your house's front door. Why not step outside and take a look at what others see? Creating a friendly front door welcomes others with a warm greeting and begins to put them at ease before you ever open the door. There are many simple ways you can make your home's exterior visually appealing with little time, effort, or money.

Painting is the most dramatic and least expensive way to decorate your front door. Does it need a fresh coat of paint? Perhaps a rich, new accent color to enhance your home's exterior? Or if you have a stained door, does it need a few coats of varnish to restore its luster? I like front doors to stand out and give a visual invitation to friends and family to "enter here." Our front door is a shiny, high-gloss, cranberry red. Every other year in the spring, I brush on a fresh coat of paint to spiff up the shine and make the door look like new. It takes little time, but gives my front door a lovely lift!

The hardware that surrounds the front door can also greatly enhance the visual appeal of a home's exterior. The most common material for exterior hardware is brass. Like gold jewelry to a sim-

ple black dress, the gleam of brass hardware gives a special sparkle and finishing touch to any front door. Brass door accessories include kick plates, knockers, light fixtures, handles, engraved name and address plaques, and house numbers. Any one of these can make your front door more attractive. When friends of ours moved into their current home years ago, the husband gave his wife a precious housewarming gift. It was a small brass plate engraved with the words "Dedicated to the Glory of God." It now humbly hangs above the brass knocker on their front door. Anyone who approaches this lovely front door knows instantly who receives the glory in their home.

There are plenty of other little touches of love that can make a home's exterior doorway beautiful. Pots or baskets of pretty flowers or plants flanking both sides of the door add color and life. Evergreen topiaries bring height and year-round greenery. Check with a local nursery to see what would be appropriate for your front door.

A pretty welcome mat can lend a friendly greeting to your front door. There are all types of beautiful, quality welcome mats available today. We have a woven, sisal welcome mat at each of our entrances. They are subtle, inexpensive, and available in several sizes and shapes. I replace them each year as the rain wears them out. I prefer the simplicity of a sisal mat, for it allows my front door and flowers to be the focal point. When selecting a welcome mat, choose one that suits your style and enhances your home's exterior.

Make sure the windows and lighting fixtures around your front door are clean and free of spider webs. Occasionally before guests arrive, I take a broom, a bottle of window cleaner, and some paper towel for a quick cleanup. It only takes a minute, but it makes my home's exterior more pleasing and presentable.

If your front door area has space, consider a pretty, weatherproof piece of furniture. It will carry the beauty and comfort of your home's interior outside and welcome others in. A pretty bench or a pair of rocking chairs visually invite visitors to have a seat and stay awhile. To protect a wood or painted finish of a piece of furniture, it is best if your entrance is under cover.

Back doors are equally, if not more important than front doors. Take a look at what you see when you walk up to your back door. If

"Whatever possessions you hold in this world — hold them with an open hand."
— Corrie ten Boom

you come home through a garage, how appealing is it? Is it filthy and filled with junk? We invest our time into what we value. Value your family and yourself by making your garage more than a greasy, grimy greeting. Take the time to get it in order. Consider staining your concrete garage floor a dark color to hide oil and dirt. Unlike paint, concrete stain won't chip or peel. Painting your garage walls a durable, semigloss white keeps it light and allows for easy cleaning.

I learned the importance of caring for my garage from my father. He has always treated his garage as if it were another room of the house. While it need not be spotless or decorated, it should be an orderly, clean, and pleasant place to come home to.

"Houses never truly sing until personal style unfolds."
— Charlotte Moss

BEAUTIFUL ENTRANCES

Whether it be a guest stepping into our home for the very first time or a loved one coming home after a long day, our entrances need to be warm and welcoming and give a preview of what lies both in our hearts and in the rooms beyond.

Express Yourself

God made you special and unique. Celebrate that uniqueness by expressing what you love in life. Begin with your entrance. One of the greatest compliments on your decorating would be for someone to enter where you live and say, "Your home is so you!" Keep in mind, you are decorating your home to reflect what you and your family enjoy. Do what you love, and don't worry what others think. If they enjoy you, they will enjoy entering and experiencing your home.

I'll never forget walking into one of my friend's homes for the first time. I had gotten to know her fairly well prior to visiting her home. I knew her heart, her passions, her personality. The minute I stepped through her front door, I knew I was at the right place. It was so Brenda — soft and pink and feminine and friendly.

Maybe you are like many of my clients who know what they like when they see it, but don't know how to express themselves in their own particular homes. I suggest you begin to discover your personal style by starting a "dream" notebook. For future reference and creative inspiration, collect pictures of rooms you love from your favorite home magazines. File the pictures by room in an accordion file or in a notebook with clear, vinyl sheet protectors. As patterns start to develop in what pleases your eye, your decorating style will unfold. I have done this for years, and although my taste has become more refined, it is amazing to see how I am consistently attracted to the same style. Once you begin to feel confident with your decorating style, introduce it in the room where most introductions occur: your entrance.

"Light is sweet, and it pleases the eyes to see the sun."
— Ecclesiastes 11:7

Let There Be Light

Light was the first element God created, and adequate lighting is a key ingredient in making a home's entrance inviting. Without proper lighting, we cannot see anything, no matter how beautiful it is. Light is energizing and welcoming. Nothing in an entrance says, "Welcome! I was expecting you!" more than a beautiful lamp lighted on a table or chest. Use a three-way bulb to alter the ambiance. When selecting lamps, consider redressing an old lamp with an updated shade and decorative finial. Or try wiring an object into a lamp — a candlestick holder, porcelain teapot, ceramic vase, or plaster statue. It saves money and gives your lamp a custom look.

My entrance lamp is made from a simple, green ceramic vase I purchased at a discount accessory store. I had it wired into a lamp, mounted on an Oriental wood base, added a silk shade, and topped it with a welcoming brass pineapple finial.

Wall treatments can also lighten up your entrances. To visually open up your entrance, paint walls a light color or wallpaper with a pattern that has a light background. If you like yellow, as I do, paint your entrance a soft, buttery yellow. It's warm, cheerful, and light and blends beautifully with most colors. Or pick a color that suits you and introduces your decorating scheme. Mirrors and glass French doors can add an appealing glimmer and reflect light. And widening your entryways into adjoining rooms can bring in tremendous amounts of light. Use decorative columns or other architectural details to enhance the openings.

Let It Flow

To gently lure friends and family into your home, your entrance should visually flow into adjacent rooms. A simple method for achieving this is to paint all doors and trim around doors and windows the same neutral color. I prefer painting all woodwork in a white, high-gloss, oil-base enamel. The high-gloss finish reflects light and gives an added sparkle to the room, and the white looks crisp and clean with all colors. Oil-base enamel is the most durable paint for woodwork throughout your home. If you prefer an off-white color for trim, use it consistently throughout your home as well.

Using similar colors can also smoothly transition your entrance into the rest of your home. I often suggest to clients just beginning to decorate their homes, or to those wanting to pull what they have together, to find a palette fabric. An artist's palette holds all the colors in his painting, even though he or she may only use one or two of those colors in one area of the painting. In the same way, your palette fabric will help you make your rooms diverse, yet still work beautifully together.

Select a palette fabric that you love for its colors, pattern, style, and texture. This fabric is primarily used in the main living area, but it will include all the colors to pull from when decorating your entire home. For example, in your entrance, use a favorite piece of artwork, a fabulous wallpaper, a hand-hooked rug in your palette colors, or a cozy wing chair covered in your palette fabric to introduce the collage of colors yet to come.

"Through knowledge its rooms are filled with rare and beautiful treasures."
— Proverbs 24:4

BEAUTIFUL LIVING ROOMS

Gone are the days when a living room was a perfectly decorated stage set for entertaining guests only. Today, whether this room is referred to as a living room, great room, family room, keeping room, den, study, or sunroom, it should be enjoyable and livable — a room that encourages us to linger. It is here that family and friends work, play, and visit, and relationships grow. Because beauty attracts, it is important that the living room be visually appealing if it is to entice us in to enjoy one another and our surroundings.

Clean It Up and Clear It Out

It is impossible to have beauty without order. Before you can bring beauty to your living room, or any room, you must first bring order to it. When you look out your window at the beautiful nature that God has created, notice the soothing sense of order. Beauty replenishes, while disorder drains. Disorder causes confusion and clutters the mind; it distracts your eyes from enjoying that which is beautiful.

Since most living rooms are the intersections for the highways of busy home life, they have a tendency to attract clutter. But be encouraged, there are simple solutions to keeping clutter under control. Endless books on organization are available today, and there are even stores that specialize in organizational products for the home. I love to use baskets to keep my home life organized. Not only are they decorative and natural-looking, they come in all sizes, shapes, and colors to suit whatever I need to store. Baskets with lids are especially attractive because they hide their contents while keeping what I need conveniently close at hand.

If organization is not one of your talents, ask an organized friend to help you get started. It's the first step toward creating a home that is pleasing to the eye.

Pretty with Paint

Once you have an idea of the feel and fabric you desire for your living room, you may want to bring out the paint brush. Paint is the easiest and least expensive way to transform your living room. With a couple of gallons of paint and a little elbow grease, any room can become light and airy, cozy and intimate, cool and soothing, or daring and dramatic. We recently painted one client's dark, paneled living room eggshell white. It has gone from being a dreary room she dreaded entering to a delightful room where she and her family love living! While we used finishing touches to keep the room warm and welcoming, the white paneling is light and gives it a crisp, clean cottage feel she adores.

As wonderful as the results of paint can be, it can be equally disastrous if the color is off. Before you break out the roller, buy a quart of your selected paint and sample it on a piece of poster board or foamcore (available in most art supply stores). Live with the color for a few days. Look at it in the daytime and nighttime. Move it around the room. I suggest using an eggshell- or satin-finish paint on walls for durability and a low sheen.

If you are extremely nervous when it comes to selecting paint color, the easiest method is to find the color you like painted in a room elsewhere and ask about it. (Keep in mind that different light levels will affect the intensity of the color.) Friends of ours recently built a new home and wanted their study walls to be eggplant purple. When the room was painted with the color they selected, it turned out to be bright purple instead. They were horrified. The wife found the color she really wanted on the walls of someone's home she visited, and now the same beautiful eggplant purple coats their walls.

"A cheerful look brings joy to the heart."
— Proverbs 15:30

A Fabulous Focal Point

For an inviting living room, find an attractive focal point and arrange your furniture around it. A focal point may be a fireplace, a bay window, or a built-in book cabinet. If your room doesn't have a focal point, create one with a cherished piece of furniture, a favorite piece of artwork, or a grouping of artifacts.

In this day and age, technology often competes for at least some of the living room spotlight. Using an entertainment center as a focal point is a beautiful solution for hiding unattractive television and stereo equipment. For a charming look, find an old linen press or armoire to use as an entertainment unit.

No matter what the weather, a fireplace can be a charming main attraction. Summerize the front of your fireplace with a decorative painted screen or a basket of flowers or plants. Warm up your mantle with whatever you love to look at — a favorite collection, a beautiful piece of artwork, a decorative mirror, a welcoming wreath. Charlotte Moss, in her book, *A Passion for Detail,* ponders the importance of the fireplace mantel as a focal point. Moss writes, "A mantel is often an easel reflecting the passions of the people who live in the house." My mantel is adorned with many picture frames filled with the faces of those I love most — my family. How can you reflect your passions around the focal point in your living room?

Whatever your focus is, it needs to be pleasing to the eye so that it will draw people in. To make your living room inviting, build the other furniture in the room around your focal point. If you have one large sofa, and space allows, consider having it directly face your focal point. If you have two loveseats, let them flank both sides of it.

There is no place more delightful than one's own fireplace.

The Warmth of Wood Furniture

When the main upholstered pieces of furniture are in place around your focal point, it's time to bring in the natural warmth and beauty of wood furniture. Determine which woods please you most and will produce the look you want to achieve. Oak and pine are casual and comfortable; walnut, cherry, and mahogany are more formal. Tastefully mix a few finishes for an eclectic look. Refinish a dull piece of old furniture to give it a rich look and luster. Add new hardware, and it looks as if you splurged on an exquisite antique!

The coffee table anchors your seating area, so be creative when you select one. Why not find an old dining table and cut down the legs? I often do this for clients to get a more unique, one-of-a-kind piece. Sturdy trunks work well too. They also give extra storage space and help keep clutter to a minimum. For additional storage and interest, use small chests as end tables.

Accent with Accessories

Accessories are the finishing touches that complete a room. Your living room is the perfect place to display accessories that please you and tell others about you. When purchasing accessories, don't buy things merely to fill up space; instead, buy only items you love. Start a collection of objects that appeal to you. A special friend of mine collects old kerosene lanterns for her cabin in the mountains. Another collects beautiful pewter pieces. Rather than scattering a collection sparingly around, display similar items together for impact. I love to collect blue and white porcelain and display several favorite pieces on a chest in our living room. Each is lovely by itself, yet when displayed together, they are far more visually appealing.

The Beauty of Books

Books lend instant warmth and beauty to any room, but especially to a living room. They invite you to sit down, curl up, and stay awhile. Often, a quick glance over the titles of the books people own can tell us much about them.

Although they can be casually displayed around a room or set in small stacks as pedestals for interesting objects, the most common way to display books is on a bookshelf or in a bookcase. When arranging books, place all hardback books together and pull their spines up flush to the edge of shelf. Stack large books horizontally on shelves or your coffee table. Place a pretty book on a plate stand and let its cover face forward on a bookshelf.

Why not make it a hobby to collect beautiful books of places you visit or things that you love? Display the books prominently in your living room, marking your favorite pictures with fabric ribbons. When you need a break, open one of the books and get lost in the beauty of the photographs. They will be a lovely reminder of your past or your passions.

"Books are beautiful things."
—George Bernard Shaw

BEAUTIFUL DINING ROOMS

Whether it be a designated room, a corner of a living room, or a kitchen table, the dining room can be any place where we sit down and slow down long enough to savor good food and fellowship. Indeed, the ritual of "breaking bread" alone can knit hearts and lives together; but the visual appeal of where we are eating can certainly add to the warmth and comfort of any occasion.

Pleasing and Practical

The first step in creating a beautiful dining room is to decide how you can best utilize the space to suit your needs, lifestyle, and tastes. There is perhaps no living space more wasted in most homes than the dining room. We often decorate our dining rooms for guests, but when guests do arrive, it's likely they will feel most at home in the rooms in which we feel most at home! Rethink the purpose of your dining room. If your living space is limited, consider letting your dining room do double duty. Fill shelves or a china cabinet with books and let your dining room serve part-time as a cozy library or study. Use a flip-top table either open for dining or closed behind a loveseat as a sofa table. Cover your dining table with pads and a tablecloth or a piece of cut glass and use it for paperwork, projects, sewing, games, or gift wrapping.

Even if space is not a problem, decorate your dining room in a style consistent with the rest of your home. A client of mine who has young children wanted to furnish her dining room in a casual, comfortable style. Rather than invest in an expensive, untouchable dining set, we furnished her dining room with an informal, but lovely table and chairs and covered her floors with woven mats of sea grass. The result was a functional and enjoyable room for her family's lifestyle.

"Don't let your possessions possess you."
— H. Jackson Brown Jr.

Marvelous Mixtures

Just as a delightful mix of personalities makes for good conversation, creative furniture combinations can liven up your dining room. Break out of the mold that says everything has to match. Intriguing rooms, like intriguing people, dare to be different. Anchor the room with a pretty table that best suits your style — a casual pine table, a rich mahogany table, or an eclectic glass top with pedestal base. Add some interesting chairs for character. If you already have a dining room set, enhance your wood chairs by alternating them with armless high-back chairs upholstered in the same fabric for unity. Or give your existing dining chairs some flair inexpensively by recovering their seats with two different, coordinating fabrics. Try wing chairs at each end of your table for coziness and height. Bring a bedroom dresser into your dining room to serve as a buffet. Tastefully mix finishes and furniture styles to delight the eye and add interest to the room. The more visually inviting your dining room is, the more you will want to use it.

Another way to add personality to your dining room is to mix dinnerware. As you collect pretty dishes and glasses, try to select things you love that work well together. Display your grandmother's priceless china alongside glass goblets you bought at a flea market. It's your home; enjoy the things you have been blessed with and mix however you wish! I have a friend who collects beautiful tea cups and saucers and uses them all at once for guests. Mixing makes the ordinary extraordinary!

If you have a silver coffee and tea service, why not break up the silver by placing the silver pieces on a bamboo or rattan tray to vary the finishes? Use a silver tray for serving a loved one breakfast in bed or place it on your bedroom dresser with a Battenburg lace doily and use it to hold perfumes and other personal items. Think creatively. When decorating your dining table, mix flower-filled terra cotta pots or wicker baskets with silver or crystal candle-holders. The eclectic combination creates a casual elegance. The eye will be intrigued as it takes in the unpredictable.

"Beauty is altogether in the eye of the beholder."
— Margaret Wolfe Hungerford

Pretty Plants

I love the natural beauty plants bring to any room. Their soothing green color reflects the peaceful outdoors, and their presence adds warmth, life, and color. Plants can also greatly enhance the dining experience. I often use them as an economical and attractive centerpiece. For a soft, lovely look, intertwine a wire wreath with ivy or overflow a basket with it. Both give a beautiful touch of graceful green without blocking the view of those seated across the table.

Many houseplants are not as difficult to grow as you might think. Some of the easiest to maintain are the Chinese evergreen, Dracaena, pothos, English ivy, parlor palm, peace plant, and philo-dendron. Invest in a few, large plants for your dining room. They fill up space and are reasonably priced.

My appreciation of plants began when I was a newlywed on a tight budget looking for inexpensive solutions to warm up our little duplex. I started with a few, small, simple pothos plants and gained confidence the longer they survived. The key to growing beautiful houseplants is consistent care. I place my plants in the shower once a week and give them a good rinse. The water feeds the plants and cleans the dust from their leaves. Once a month I fertilize them with plant food. When their leaves have dried after watering, I mist them with leaf polish to give them a shiny, healthy look. (The spray is available in most garden centers or hardware stores.) I now love growing plants in my home, and while they are having their weekly shower, my rooms seem lifeless without them!

I prefer using real plants and greenery. If, however, live plants just aren't your thing, quality artificial ones are an alternative. They are more expensive than real plants, but they are virtually carefree and can still bring beauty and warmth to your home.

The Loveliness of Lighting

A dining room's ambiance can be greatly altered by lighting. Lighting in a dining room should be subtle, but adequate to see your food and the faces of those with whom you are dining. Certainly, the spirit of the event determines how bright the lighting should be: the calmer the atmosphere, the dimmer the lighting.

A candle can pierce the darkest night.

If you have a chandelier in your dining room, install a dimmer switch to allow you to vary the mood. I suggest installing dimmers in any room where you want greater control with your overhead lighting: your front hallway, kitchen, or powder room. To enhance a dining room chandelier, consider topping off its bulbs with miniature shades. Available in many colors and styles, they add a finishing touch to your center-stage lighting. For a custom look, spray or handpaint shades or cover them in fabric or paper and finish them off with trim. Many lighting stores will also customize lampshades by covering them in whatever you desire. Soften the look of the chain link on your chandelier by covering it with a shirred sleeve of fabric.

The glitter of candlelight is always a beautiful way to light a dining table. Cluster pretty candlesticks with colorful, lighted candles on your table. I collect brass candlesticks in all sizes and shapes and often use them on my dining table to light up an evening. For a touch of elegance on an extra-special occasion, use eighteen-inch candles.

Often when we sit down to dinner, I dim the lights and light a candle at our table. I find it helps calm our minds and hearts so we can enjoy our meal and one another. Such a small gesture takes little effort, yet makes such a difference in the atmosphere of a meal. Even if you live alone, treat yourself to the ambiance of a little candlelight. Savor the beauty of the simple things in life.

Other touches of light can enhance the ambiance of your dining room as well. Place a spotlight on the floor behind a plant in a corner or behind a folding screen. The shadows cast on the walls will add visual appeal. If you have a painting, a picture light will bring the colors and depth of your artwork to life.

Mirrors can also make a dining room enchanting, sending out touches of light as they reflect whatever is in the room. I love the look of candle flames flickering in a mirror. Find an old, large frame and have a beveled mirror cut for it to enhance a dining room wall. Or collect a variety of smaller, interesting mirrors and hang them together in a collage. Years ago, we came across a large piece of artwork in a lovely, antique gold frame. Though the artwork didn't suit our style, we loved the frame, so we had an inexpensive piece of mirror cut to fill the frame. The beautiful, framed mirror now adorns a wall in our home. Though it looks priceless, it cost very little.

BEAUTIFUL KITCHENS

Though the primary function of the kitchen is to prepare food to feed our stomachs, feasting our eyes on all the beauty a kitchen holds can be equally satisfying. An attractive kitchen is one that is cheerful, functional, and beautiful — cheerful in that it is light-filled and makes us happy to be there; functional in that what we fill it with is convenient and can be used in the storage, preparation, or serving of food; and beautiful in that what we surround ourselves with is lovely to look at. Keep these three qualities in mind as you make decisions for new purchases for your kitchen or when sorting through those things which you already have.

"Sight is a faculty; seeing is an art."
— George Perkins

Charming Cabinets

Built-in cabinets have not always been a standard kitchen ingredient. Originally, separate pieces of furniture were used for food storage and preparation. Over time, custom cabinets and countertops were developed to provide maximum space efficiency. Though the benefits of such modern inventions are bountiful, much of the charm of the kitchen has been lost because of them. Built-in cabinets often look sterile and can dominate a great deal of the wall space in a kitchen. There are, however, beautiful touches that can warm up your kitchen cabinets. The key is to visually break up the span of cabinets, giving your eye something interesting to take in other than a wall of wood.

One of the simplest ways to add character to your kitchen cabinets is updating your hinges and knobs. Try color-coordinating the knobs to match your kitchen colors and accessories. Ceramic knobs come in a rainbow of colors. A client of mine has a beautiful blue-and-white kitchen. After we gave her cabinets a fresh coat of glossy, white, oil-base paint, we added blue ceramic knobs. They were the perfect finishing touch.

Another option is to replace a few cabinet doors that are in a visible and convenient location with glass doors. Display your dinnerware, accessories, and glassware here. For a charming cottage look that hides your cabinet contents, consider window-framed cabinet doors lined with shirred fabric rather than glass. Or save time and money and simply remove the doors of a few cabinets and paint the interiors, using the open shelving to show off your tableware.

Dear friends of ours recently built a house. To keep within their budget, they decided to forego glass doors on their kitchen cabinets; instead, they had open shelving built between two sets of cabinets. What seemed to be a sacrifice turned out to be a beautiful blessing! The shelves provide a delightful nook to store Kay's darling teapot collection.

Appealing Appliances

Most contemporary kitchens today contain convenient appliances to help make food preparation as efficient and enjoyable as possible. More and more, products are being manufactured that are not only very functional, but also quite attractive.

Ideally, appliances should visually coordinate with the rest of your kitchen. If your current major kitchen appliances don't match, use epoxy paint to coordinate them. If you don't want to do it your-

"Look at everything as though you were seeing it either for the first or last time. Then your time on earth will be filled with glory."
— Betty Smith

self, there are paint experts who will come to your home and refinish your appliances to give them a brand new look. Although not as durable as the original manufacturer's baked-on enamel, these finishes are less expensive than replacing appliances that function fine. We have done this in our home. Remodeling costs can run high, and the cost of a new major appliance is not always a priority.

If you have an electric stove top, beautify your burners (when not in use) with enameled cooktop covers. They are available in several colors to coordinate with your kitchen. Not only do they save clean-up chores, they also create extra workspace while hiding unattractive burners. Coordinate the front of your dishwasher with your kitchen by slipping an inexpensive piece of laminate in its place. For an extra touch, handpaint something special on it.

Make the front of your refrigerator a sight to be seen. Clear everything off of your refrigerator doors—emergency phone numbers, magnets, and whatever else is hanging around. Instantly, your kitchen will look cleaner and fresher. Hang an attractive bulletin board to hold important information and priceless pieces of homemade artwork in an unobtrusive, but convenient spot. If you want to use your refrigerator to display things, make it look as pleasant as possible and edit it often. Remember, you cannot have beauty without order. Use clear, acrylic, magnetic frames to display photos of family and friends.

Countertop clutter can be a real eyesore when it comes to kitchen beauty. Display utensils and portable appliances that are beautiful and often used; store those that are purely functional. If it's time for a new appliance such as a coffeemaker or toaster oven, consider an under-the-counter model. It will give your kitchen a cleaner look and increase your work space.

Functional Furniture

If there is a corner in your kitchen that needs a touch of charm, fill it with a baker's rack or some other unique piece of furniture. Both can be used to store kitchen necessities, such as cookbooks or other items that need to be close at hand. When selecting a piece of furniture for your kitchen, however, be certain it is useful for your particular needs and suits your sense of style.

"Don't be afraid to do things with flair . . . Flair is a creative expression God has imprinted on our souls."
— Karen Mains

The first piece of furniture Bill and I ever purchased is our most prized possession: an old Victorian hutch. We found this treasure on sale for eighty dollars in a candy shop that was going out of business. It now has a prominent place along one of our kitchen walls. This graceful hutch stores kitchen necessities behind its doors, while sharing beauty and preserving memories on the outside.

Other furniture that can be beautiful and functional are your kitchen table and chairs. If you have an old kitchen table and chairs that need a lift, why not paint them a pleasing color with oil-based paint? Counter stools can also add flexibility and function to a kitchen. Add a custom touch by painting them or adding pretty seat cushions.

"Have nothing in your homes that you do not know to be useful and believe to be beautiful."
— William Morris

Attractive Accessories

In any room, but especially in the kitchen, accessories need to be both accessible to the hand and enjoyable to the eye. Kitchen counter space is often limited, so it's important to keep fragile decorative accessories out of the way. To solve this challenge, try displaying decorative kitchen items on your walls. Hang a simple shelf across a doorway or window and load it up with decorative kitchen objects you love, but use less frequently. If you have young children, this will also keep breakable items within view but out of reach of curious little hands.

Decorative plates can be used many different ways in the kitchen. Prop them on stands on a shelf or hutch, hang them with wire hangers that slip onto the back of the plate, or mount them on a brass strip or iron rod that holds several plates at a time. If you need to use them, just take them down and rinse them off!

Pot racks are also perfect for displaying beautiful, but necessary cookware. One client of mine collects copper. Her pot rack is overflowing with lovely copper pieces that she uses to cook or display food. When not in use, the pieces' beautiful copper finish brings warmth to her cozy kitchen.

Baskets are a practical and pretty way to enhance your kitchen decor. I stack them on top of my refrigerator. If you have space above your kitchen cabinets, display baskets there to lend warmth and beauty to your kitchen. I love baskets so much that my kitchen trash can is a large, lidded, wicker hamper. If space under your sink is tight, or you simply want a larger trash can, consider using one like mine. It holds a substantial amount of trash, so it needs to be emptied less frequently (Bill loves it too!). I got this idea from a special friend of mine, Sandra Stanley. If you see a friend doing something in her home that you love, let it inspire you. Imitation is the greatest compliment!

Find creative and beautiful ways to display food items in your kitchen. Store flour, sugar, coffee, and tea in lovely canisters. Use a pretty cookie jar to stash cookies. Display colorful pastas in over-size glass containers. Fill colored or clear glass bottles with flavored oils and vinegars. Overflow a bowl with one type of fruit. My mother loves to collect handmade pottery for her kitchen. Each piece is pleasing to her eye and useful in her kitchen. A sugar bowl and creamer, a lidded butter dish, or a milk pitcher can all display food with a sense of pleasure.

"If you wisely invest in beauty, it will remain with you all the days of your life."
— Frank Lloyd Wright

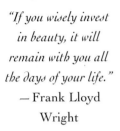

BEAUTIFUL BEDROOMS

The bedroom is the first and last place we see every day. It is our own private world—where we retreat to find rest, love, comfort, and health. Here we are replenished and strengthened for another day of life on earth. Because of these things, it is important that we make our bedrooms intimate, cozy, romantic, and most of all, beautiful. As we do, we will be drawn to them. And as we are drawn to them, they will help us bring balance back into our lives.

Beautiful Beds

My sentiments regarding the importance of a beautiful bed are reflected in the well-worded Thomasville Furniture ad which profoundly states, "A bed should never be so boring that it puts you to sleep." A beautiful bed should take center stage in the bedroom. It is, after all, the main reason you are in the room. Place your bed in a spot where you can enjoy the greatest view while lying in it. If room allows, consider putting it at an angle in a corner. What style of bed best reflects your personality? If at all possible, save your money and treat yourself to a beautiful, quality bed that you can enjoy for the rest of your life.

Many people like the romantic look of a four-poster bed. I love the look of a high bed several feet off the ground. Friends of ours are saving for a four-poster bed, but meanwhile they have placed their current bed on sturdy, wood blocks to raise it higher and give it a more romantic feel.

Dressing your bed in a pleasing way greatly enhances your bedroom. For a touch of romance, soften your bed with a valance or canopy or fabric draped behind it. When I was a little girl, my mother decorated my sister's and my bedroom in pink and white gingham. Then she crowned each of our twin beds with sweet little canopies by simply stitching a rod pocket at the top and bottom of a strip of fabric and shirring it onto two curtain rods with different size returns. It didn't take much time or fabric for my mother to bring a touch of beauty to our bedroom, and we felt like princesses!

"She makes coverings for her bed."
— Proverbs 31:22

Mixing and matching fabrics can make beds visually interesting. I love floral fabrics; they bring the beauty, color, and pattern of God's creation inside. Florals mixed with other simpler patterns in similar colors are a smashing combination. Try plaids, checks, stripes, geometrics, or textured solids as mix-and-match fabrics. Many manufacturers today are taking the guesswork out of decorating by making beautiful, ready-made bed ensembles in a tasteful mixture of fabrics.

Be on the lookout for reasonably-priced fabric remnants. Many of the fabrics I use to mix and match for clients, as well as for myself, are remnants. They are usually the end of bolts or dye lots so the yardage available is limited and seldom enough to use as a main fabric to decorate a room, but remnants work great as complementary fabrics. God has provided beautiful fabrics at unbelievable prices for clients on shoestring budgets!

Double up on your decorating by making or buying a duvet cover that has a different fabric on each side. Flip it when it is soiled or simply for a new look. Layer your dust ruffle to give it a deluxe designer touch. Use one long and one short dust ruffle, or, if the two are the same size, simply pull up on the top one and pin it to your box spring. The results will be beautiful whether you have a standard or a high bed.

For a client's master bedroom, I recently made a top dust ruffle in green-and-white check and the underlying ruffle in Battenburg lace that had been a table runner. The lace added a touch of romance to the casual check. Keep in mind when dressing your bed that the dust ruffle need not touch the floor if your bed frame is attractive.

Pillows are a perfect way to dress up your bed and make it inviting. When piling on pillows, use an eclectic mix of different shapes, sizes, colors, and fabrics for visual interest. Give a ready-made pillow a custom look by tying it with a decorative tassel or fabric bow.

One final note on creating a beautiful bed. As I have stated, you cannot have beauty without order. It is essential that you make your bed if it is to be beautiful. Try to establish a habit of making your bed as you leave it in the morning, and teach your family to do the same. Certainly, there are occasions when an unmade bed feels carefree. But more often than not, this simple task will set the tone for your day. A wonderful friend of ours, Dave Wilson, is an excellent swimmer who once dreamed of competing in the Olympics. While struggling with discipline during his training, Dave's coach asked him if he made his bed in the morning. Dave said he did not. His coach suggested he start his discipline training the minute he rolled out of his bed by making it. His efforts paid off. Making his bed was not all Dave made. He went on to participate in the 1984 Olympics and won both gold and silver medals in swimming.

Bedside Beauty

Along with a beautiful bed, it is important to make the bedside both functional and visually appealing. If you have a bedroom set with two nightstands, consider breaking up the pair. Variety is the spice of life! A tasteful mixture of bedside furnishings will make your bedroom more pleasing to the eye.

Replace one end table with a round skirted table or other interesting piece. I often use a wood nightstand on a man's bedside and go for a softer, more feminine, skirted table on a woman's side. A skirted table is an economical way to add warmth, color, and coziness

"Creating beautiful things is how women have spoken of their love and heritage since the beginning of time."
— Anita Luvera Mayer

to any room and give great out-of-sight but close-at-hand storage. For a custom look, embellish the bottom of a table skirt with cording, fringe, shirred fabric, banding, or a ruffle. Top the skirted table with a lace or square fabric overlay and a piece of cut glass.

Once you have your bedside furniture in place, beautify the room with objects that are necessary *and* lovely to look at. Use a small basket beside your bed to organize pens, paper, address book, and other items you desire, or place pens and pencils in a small, pretty vase. Store magazines and books in a larger, lidded wicker basket on the floor beside your bed. The less clutter, the more peaceful your bedroom will be.

Adequate lighting is very important to the enjoyment of a bedroom, yet it is an element that is often overlooked. To keep bedside tables clear, swing arm lamps are a lovely solution. Customize with a beautiful shade or try converting silver-plated candleholders into candlestick lamps and top them with a small, silk shade. Candlestick lamps give height and light without taking much room from your bedside table. For a touch of color, tie a tassel around the lamp neck. If possible, install recessed lighting over your bed and place it on a dimmer. This will allow you to enhance light for reading or dim it to set a romantic ambiance.

"You, O LORD, keep my lamp burning; my God turns my darkness into light."
— Psalm 18:28

Adorning Accessories

The accessories we choose to adorn our bedrooms with should be especially pleasing to our eyes and close to our heart. When selecting artwork, pick something that you love or that carries special meaning. Rather than hanging one picture over the bed, consider stacking two pairs of smaller artwork for interest. Or make your bedroom personal and intimate by dressing your dresser with pretty picture frames filled with the faces of those you love.

Use items creatively. My favorite accessory in our bedroom is my jewelry box. It is a mahogany box that has flowers handpainted on its lid. Although it is lovely to look at, what pleases me most is that it was actually my grandmother's silver chest. I transformed it into something I needed and can enjoy seeing as I open it every day. What hidden treasures are tucked away in your attic that could be used to adorn your bedroom?

The Wonder of Windows

The primary purpose of windows is to bring the light, air, and beauty of the outdoors into your room. While window treatments should enhance the room and provide privacy, it is important to not cover the windows, thereby losing these natural, essential ingredients to healthy living. The possibilities for window fashion are as limitless as clothing fashion. I prefer simple window treatments. Shutters or wood blinds that match window trim are subtle, yet allow for privacy when needed. Matchstick wood blinds are reasonably priced and give a natural, woven appearance. They can be rolled up to enjoy a full view or rolled down for complete privacy. Roller shades can be customized with fabric and trim. Simple lace panels shirred on wood or iron rods are delicate and soothing to the eye. Fabric top treatments or side panels add softness and color. There are also many ready-made window treatments on the market. But remember, however you choose to treat your windows, keep them consistent with your decorating style.

"The heavens declare the glory of God; the skies proclaim the work of his hands."
— Psalm 19:1

BEAUTIFUL BATHROOMS

Soaking in the bathtub provides us with a moment of stillness to look around and evaluate life. As you look around your bathroom, do you like what you see? The average person will spend seven years of their life in the bathroom, so no matter how big or small, it should be a private place that accommodates your personal needs while pleasing your eyes. Enjoying a lovely bathroom need not require a major renovation. A few simple touches can enhance this room greatly.

Bathroom Basics

Because you cannot have beauty without order, keeping a bathroom clean and orderly is the first step to making it pleasing to the eye. Since the bathroom is where we clean our bodies, there are many products and appliances that are used to help us look our best.

Store beauty products, hair dryers, and curling appliances when not in use. In fact, the more you reduce countertop clutter in your bathroom, the easier it will be to wipe down and keep clean. If cabinet space is limited, add a touch of charm and storage with a pretty piece of furniture such as a dainty chest or wicker cabinet. I have a white wicker double shelf in my guest bathroom that holds decorative, cork-topped glass bottles filled with mouthwash, bubble bath, and lotions. The colorful liquids are lovely to look at, within easy reach for any guest, and help to make them feel at home.

"Blessed are the eyes that see what you see."
— Luke 10:23

For a beautiful touch to a bathroom sink, transform an old-fashioned washstand or small chest into a stylish vanity by having a plumber install a decorative basin sink into it. I have done this for clients and it adds warmth and charm, especially for a powder room.

A large mirror over your sink can expand and enhance a bathroom. Trim out the mirror around your sink with decorative wood molding to give it a custom look. Our current master bathroom was cozy and comfortable, but we wanted to open it up visually, so, behind our sink, we had mirror cut from the top of the counter to the ceiling. The bathroom's size hasn't changed a bit, but it now appears twice as big. In addition to mirrors, be sure you have adequate lighting in your bathroom. If possible, install recessed lighting and place it on a dimmer switch to vary your bathroom atmosphere.

To keep your bathroom looking beautiful, wall treatments need to be selected with care. Consider painting walls with enamel paint or choose a vinyl-coated wallpaper that is durable and can withstand heat and moisture. Save more fragile wallpaper for your powder room. If you lease where you live and are unable to paint or hang wallpaper, consider hanging a decorative border using plastic tack that adheres to walls without damaging them. It will help you give your home a little touch of your own.

Little Luxuries

Little luxuries can make your bathroom beautiful. Bring splashes of color into your bathroom with pretty towels and throw rugs that coordinate with your decorating scheme. Don't stash your color in a closet — store your bath towels on pegs of a wall rack painted to coordinate with your colors. If an update is due, change your towel bar and toilet tissue holder to more decorative ones.

Have a pretty night-light in each of your bathrooms. These can be reassuring for children, guests, and even yourself. Use natural objects, like seashells, to hold soap bars or jewelry beside your bathroom sink. Have a pretty cup and soap dish or dispenser adorn your sink.

I love to use wicker baskets in my bathrooms. I use natural-colored, round, wicker trash cans everywhere and place a fresh paper doily in the bottom of each. Place a pretty basket beside your toilet to hold current magazines.

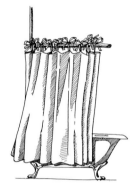

Treat your eyes and your bathroom to a pretty, new shower curtain. Tie grosgrain bows to each plastic ring to give it some punch. When decorating a bathroom on a budget, I often hang a standard Battenburg lace shower curtain. To give it color and a custom touch, I tie big fabric bows to the rings out of the same fabric that is being used for the window treatments. If your bathroom windows need privacy, but you want to enjoy maximum sunlight, sew a rod pocket on a Battenburg tablecloth. Shirr it on a wood rod in front of the window high enough for privacy, but still allowing for your window to be partially exposed. The sunlight will filter through the cuttings in the fabric. The white cotton fabric won't fade, and its simplicity and beauty will enhance any bathroom decor.

Tiny Thought

Lord,
Open my eyes,
Help me to see
The blessings of beauty
You've created for me.

Tips for Pleasing the Eye

Begin a "my favorite things" box. Use a decorative shoe box or hatbox to collect favorite items like trims, fabric swatches, ribbons, paper napkins, stationery, or other colorful memorabilia. This box will help you discover the most appealing color scheme for your home.

Be on the lookout. Observation is one of the best ways to train your eyes and learn what pleases you most. Tour model homes. Wander through furniture showrooms. Visit decorator showhouses. Go on home tours. Take your camera and a notebook, documenting anything you love.

Compromise on spotlessness. Arrive at a practical balance for cleanliness and sanity. Clean as you go. If things are orderly and lovely to look at, a little dust or dirt won't be as distracting.

Begin with something beautiful. If you are wondering where to start to make a room pleasing to the eye, begin with what you have and love. Then work your way up, starting with the floor, furniture, walls, windows, and, finally, accessories.

Try it before you buy it. Before buying yards of fabric or rolls of wallpaper, put the pattern on trial. Tape a large sample of your selection to a wall in the room in which you plan to use it. By looking at it and living with it for several days or weeks, you will be better able to determine if the pattern is right for you, possibly avoiding a costly mistake.

Move it! Rearrange furniture for a new look, making sure your favorite pieces are placed in positions for you to enjoy.

Store memories by the bowlful. Put a big bowl or basket on your coffee table and fill it with family photos that haven't yet been filed into albums.

Keep it fresh with flowers. Bring God's bountiful beauty into your home with a colorful bouquet of flowers. Make it a ritual when you go the grocery store or farmer's market to pick up a bunch. Select those that appeal to you and go with your color scheme. They will lift your spirits as they please your eyes.

Chapter Three

~

Fragrancing
Your Home

And the house was filled with the
fragrance of the perfume.
John 12:3

A Hint of Scent

As a young girl, visiting my godmother, Sophie, was one of my childhood highlights. It was always a scent-filled experience. Her home was filled with a unique, yet pleasant fragrance of mothballs, perfume, and food cooking. The writing desk that now fills our home was once Sophie's. To this day, when I open one of the drawers, a whiff of its interior takes me back to her home years ago.

One of God's sweetest gifts to us is our sense of smell. Similarly, one of the most satisfying things we can share with those who enter our homes is pleasant fragrance. Fragrance is a gift that will gratify today and linger in our memories long after it is gone.

Whether we notice it or not, fragrance fills our lives. Every breath we take brings the opportunity to whiff something wonderful. God created human noses in all sizes and shapes, but each serves the same primary purpose — to enable us to breathe and smell. Most noses can detect up to ten thousand different smells! Unfortunately, it seems the only scents we stop and smell, pleasant or unpleasant, are those that are especially strong.

The well-known saying, "Take time to smell the roses," suggests we slow our lives down enough to relish the goodness of life through the simple smells that surround us: fresh-cut grass, lemon-polished furniture, ripe strawberries, freshly shampooed hair, charcoal steak on the grill, or clothesline-fresh laundry. God has given us all these aromas to enjoy. I hope the following pages on fragrance will inspire you to smell the "roses" already in your life and add some new blossoms to your fragrant bouquet.

Selecting Scents

When selecting scents, keep in mind that their purpose is to enhance your home, not overpower it. A few, simple touches in each room are all you need. Fragrances are classified in many different ways, but household products basically come in five main

"One of nature's most bountiful gifts is the aura of aroma."
— Karol DeWulf Nickel

types of scents. When selecting fragrances for each room, I try to keep a theme. I prefer floral or fruity fragrances in the warmer months and spicy or woodsy scents in the cooler months. And I enjoy herbal scents all year long, especially in my kitchen and bathroom. You can breathe easy, however; there are no rules. Instead, let your nose be the judge of what is pleasant and appropriate for your home.

As lovely as many fragrances are, none will last forever. The longevity of each scent depends on the original quality of the fragrance and where you place it. If a fragrant product is placed near heat, moisture, or circulating air, its scent will be short and sweet. It will smell potent, but all of its scent particles will be quickly diffused into the air. If, however, a fragrance is placed in a cool, dry, closed area, like a closet or a drawer, its scent will be released more slowly. As with any blessing in life, enjoy each fragrance while it lasts.

Fragrance Stirs Emotions

Proverbs 27:9 puts it perfectly: "Perfume and incense bring joy to the heart." Smelling a pleasant fragrance gives life a little lift. The reason smells have such a deep emotional effect on us is that God, in his goodness, wired up our noses to our brains in such a way that the slightest smell can stir our souls. When we inhale a fragrance, it goes straight from the nerve endings in our nostrils to our forebrain, the part of the brain that deals with emotions, instincts, and urges. Because of this, smell, while perhaps the least intellectual, is possibly the most influential sense we possess.

Smells can stir up a myriad of emotions. They can relax you, remind you, repulse you, soothe you, seduce you, excite you, entice you, invigorate you, or invite you. Think of walking into a beautiful, fragrant gift shop. Doesn't it make you want to linger for hours? Or how about the smell of roasting turkey on Thanksgiving? Doesn't it make you feel secure, even cozy?

Different scents can also arouse different emotional responses. Vanilla reduces stress. Lemon wakes you up. Peppermint enhances your concentration. Pine and cedar soothe you. Rose and myrrh make you feel romantic. Lavender and chamomile make you sleepy.

"Smells are surer than sounds and sights to make your heartstrings crack."
— Rudyard Kipling

Research indicates that some scents can sweeten sour dispositions and even reduce aggression. It also shows that women perceive and respond to odors more than men, perhaps because God designed us to be more tuned in to and sensitive to our surroundings. Whatever the reason, scenting our homes can be one of the secrets women have to stir the emotions of those who live there.

Fragrance Makes Memories

Isn't it interesting that a breath of something familiar can instantly carry your mind to another time, another place? And when a fragrance takes you back in time, you recall not only the scent, but a whole scene. The smell of honeysuckle always transports me to the woods beside the playground of my elementary school. I can visualize it in crystal-clear detail. It is here in this place that I, along with my girlfriends, played my favorite pastime — house. We would sweep the dirt floors with pine branch broomsticks and suck the sweet nectar out of the tiny, fragrant honeysuckle blossoms. The honeysuckle nourished our noses more than our stomachs; maybe that's why I remember it so well, and why, with a whiff of it even now, I am twice blessed. This year, I plan to plant a honeysuckle bush in my backyard. Though I'm no longer a child, its scent will keep me young at heart. What are some pleasant fragrances you recall from your childhood? Are there simple ways you can bring that scent into your home to enjoy again?

"Smell is a potent wizard that transports us across thousands of miles and all the years we have lived."
— Helen Keller

God has given us a built-in memory maker with our sense of smell. Stimulating it, we have a powerful tool that will tug our family's heartstrings toward home. Twenty years from now others may not remember the fabric that covered your sofa. They most likely won't recall the food you cooked for dinner last week. But if you fill your home with a bounty of fragrance, I assure you they will carry those memories with them long after the scent is gone. Leave them a legacy of love by filling their noses, hearts, and minds with delightful fragrances. It will be well worth your while.

Fragrance Satisfies

Smell is one of the easiest senses to stimulate in the home with, perhaps, the greatest reward. A woman who had attended one of my workshops was discouraged that her husband seldom noticed anything she did in the home. She came to me several weeks later thrilled over her husband's response to her scent experiment. He was reading the newspaper in his usual position and focused manner when he stopped, put down the paper, and inquired where the pleasant smell was coming from. She had placed a scented ring in the lamp by his chair! Often, the simplest things in life can bring the greatest sense of satisfaction.

When selecting scents to fill your home, experiment with different fragrances to discover which ones satisfy you and those with whom you live. Although women prefer floral fragrances, men often like spicy smells. If you are married, think of some creative ways you can surprise your husband and "add a little spice" to his home life.

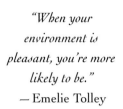

"When your environment is pleasant, you're more likely to be."
— Emelie Tolley

Fragrance Today

Today, fragrances are all around us. You can sprinkle them, spray them, hang them, heat them, pour them, place them, plug them, shower in them, and scrub with them. The fragrance business is blossoming like never before as manufacturers, recognizing the allure of fragrance, are enjoying the sweet smell of success by scenting every product possible. Many magazines contain peel-and-smell strips that reveal the hottest perfume fragrances. The art of aromatherapy confirms the interest in smell and its effect on our emotions, mood, and behavior.

Of all fragrances, home fragrance products are the most profitable. Amazingly, only twenty percent of the profits of the perfume industry come from fragrancing body scents. Eighty percent come from fragrancing household products — everything from cleaning products to paper products. The bottom line? Smell sells, especially when it comes to our homes.

The vast array of home fragrance products on the market makes it easy to fill our homes with herbs and spice and everything nice. There are many doable and buyable ideas for bringing fragrance to our homes with little effort. The contemporary woman has fragrance at her fingertips.

FRAGRANT EXTERIORS

To make your home fragrant and alluring, begin with its exterior. A fragrant wreath or bouquet on your front door is a sure way to welcome loved ones. I often hang a colorful, dried floral wreath on my front door. Dried flowers are beautiful and long-lasting, but they are scentless. (Flowers lose their fragrance when dehydrated.) To refresh the floral fragrance, I just dab a few drops of essential or refresher oil on the wreath's dried leaves. This fragrant oil is highly concentrated and comes in many lovely scents.

For a special occasion, tuck a few sweet-smelling flowers, like roses or daffodils, in a fresh wreath of greenery. Ready-made wreaths can be found at garden centers, farmers markets, and floral shops. Try using a eucalyptus wreath. Eucalyptus is among the most aromatic plants in the world because of its refreshing scent. Add a hint of sea lavender to soften the look, and you instantly have an invigorating and inviting door that will tempt any nose to enter.

Fragrant flowers blooming from baskets, pots, or watering cans also lend warmth and pleasant scent to your home's exterior. I love the smell of geraniums. Although it is primarily the leaves that give these flowering plants their unique scent, geraniums have enhanced homes for years. In Victorian homes, pots of geraniums were placed up the sides of the front stairway. As women passed by the pots, their long skirts would brush against the flowers, releasing the geranium's fragrant perfume. Geraniums planted in simple terra cotta pots can make a sunny exterior friendly and fragrant. In winter, bring the pots indoors to a cheery spot. Their scent will remind the winter-weary soul that spring is just around the corner.

This past summer, I was attending an evening Bible study in a lovely Atlanta home. The gracious hostess had placed highly fragrant citronella candles outside to burn at her front and back doors. These candles are a great scent-filled solution to fragrancing your home's exterior while keeping warm-weather bugs on the run.

"The blossoming vines spread their fragrance."
— Song of Songs
2:13

When planting flowers or shrubbery outside your home, consider those that are aromatic as well as attractive. As I said, my favorite fragrant shrub is the sweet-smelling honeysuckle. I'm not the only one that loves it; hummingbirds and butterflies swarm to its nectar-filled blooms. The beautiful butterfly bush attracts bystanders and butterflies with its colorful cones of fragrant flowers. My sister, Kelly, who lives three doors down from me, fills her beautiful window boxes with fragrant annuals.

Our mailbox post is covered with jasmine vines. They grow wonderfully in the mild Georgia weather. In the spring, summer, and fall, the free-flowing vines are covered with tiny, fragrant flowers that make stepping outside to collect the mail a sweet treat. Think of one corner of the world outside your front door that could be enhanced with fragrance. Check with your local garden center for suggestions. Let fragrance bloom where you have planted it!

"The complex aroma of a home is inimitable. Nothing else smells like home."
— Janine King

FRAGRANT ENTRANCES

What better place to begin thinking about fragrance than the first place that welcomes visitors from the outside — your entrance. While their eyes are busy taking in the scenery, their noses are just as rapidly taking in the scents. From the initial smell, an indelible impression about your home is being made in the brain of the beholder. Take advantage of this wonderful opportunity to greet family and friends by fragrancing your home's entrance in a pleasant way.

The first house Bill and I owned was a small ranch home in Texas. The house had been on the market for quite a while before we purchased it. I strongly believe it had not sold primarily because of the strong smell that hit you the minute you walked in. It was putrid. Other prospective buyers probably never made it past the front door.

A Step Inside

All the fragrances we use indoors originate outdoors. So, the first scent of the first step inside should be as fresh and natural as possi-

ble. Display at least one fragrant object of nature on your entrance table. For a fresh fruit smell, fill a bowl with all apples, lemons, or limes. For a floral fragrance, cluster sweet-smelling daffodils in a pretty vase. For a bit of spice, brim a basket with scented pinecones. All are simple to do. All smell wonderful. All say welcome.

If you are just beginning to discover the satisfaction of scenting your home, start with a lamp ring. Your entrance is the perfect spot to experiment. Whoever enters will enjoy your home's smell, even if they never get past the foyer! Place the ring on a cool lightbulb in a table lamp in your entrance. Before turning the lightbulb on, add a few drops of a favorite essential oil. The heat of the bulb will diffuse the pleasant fragrance throughout the room for hours.

If you want to be greeted by a pleasant-smelling home, set your lamp (with drops of oil already in its ring) on a timer so that it will turn on several minutes before you expect to arrive. The minute you walk in, the smell will catch you by surprise and warm your heart.

Scented lamp rings are one of my favorite methods to fragrance the home because they are safe and easy. If you have young children, they are a wonderful way to keep fragrance in the air, but out of the way of little hands. I now have rings on lamps throughout my home. Often before friends or family arrive, I scurry around with a bottle of essential oil, dotting a few drops of liquid fragrance in each ring. In minutes, my whole home smells like the flowers of spring, or the apples and cinnamon of fall, or the evergreen scent of winter. Fill your lamp ring with a fragrance you fancy.

Recently, I had several women visiting my home for the first time. After walking around, one of the women curiously asked where the wonderful smell was hiding. It was in the lamp rings! I sometimes keep extra lamp rings on hand as favors. That day, I bid my new friends farewell with a new way for them to fragrance their own homes.

Scented candles can also enhance any room of your home. Place them where the people will be, so the fragrance can be enjoyed. I find the sparkle and smell of a scented candle to be a warm greeting that always says "home." If you are expecting friends, light a large scented candle in your front entrance. You can also cluster small

"To keep a lamp burning, we have to keep putting oil in it."
— Mother Teresa

votive candles, entwined with sprigs of ivy, on a decorative tray and place them on a chest in your entrance. Both are fragrant ways to welcome others. I don't save scented candles for just my front-door friends. In the evening, I often light a scented candle by the back door to let family or friends know I am expecting them.

Scented candles must be very fragrant and made well in order to serve their purpose. Let your nose be your guide when selecting scented candles. If a candle smells strong without being lit, it is apt to have a fragrance that lasts while burning. Whenever possible, purchase scented candles instead of unscented candles. For a few pennies more, you can enjoy stimulating two senses instead of one. If, however, you have an unscented votive candle or large pillar candle, adding a few drops of essential oil below the wick before burning will release the fragrance when lit. The fragrance will last as long as the oil does.

Fragrancing your entrance also includes fragrancing yourself in a way that is pleasing to those you love. Keep a small bottle of perfume in a basket near the entrance where you usually greet your family. A quick spray will refresh you and welcome those you love with a sweet aroma well worth coming home to.

The fragrances that fill our homes today will be the memories that fill our minds tomorrow.

The Coat Closet

Whenever your friends or family enter your home wearing coats or other outerwear, they will, more than likely, use your coat closet. Given the nature of its purpose, a coat closet may sometimes smell stale, damp, or musty. What a perfect opportunity for an unexpected scent of freshness! Use cedar hangers to hang coats and jackets. Cedar is one of God's most amazing woods. It contains natural aromatics that repel moths and mildew while absorbing moisture and mustiness. And it smells as fresh as a forest!

You can also enhance the scent of your coat closet by tucking a cedar block or a pleasing sachet on the top shelf. I have a lovely gardenia sachet envelope in my coat closet. Even though I know it's there, it seems the floral scent catches me by surprise every time I swing open the door.

FRAGRANT LIVING ROOMS

The living room is a place for gathering and making others feel welcome and comfortable. Because fragrance has a powerful effect on our emotions and behavior, a pleasant fragrance in the living room can help make it a place where friends and family can relax.

The living room usually has wide spans of open area, several pieces of furniture, and maybe even a fireplace. All are wonderful spots from which to disperse delightful perfumes. The living room is the place we usually sit and stay in for more than a mere moment, the one room where we can truly enjoy living as we take in our fragrant surroundings.

"One's home should smell as beautiful as it looks."
— Barbara Milo Ohrbach

Fresh Air

Before we fill our living rooms with fragrance, we may need to clear the air that already fills them. Unpleasant smells from pets, lingering food, or mildew are bound to occur in most any household. On a mild day, open your windows and let the breeze sweep through the living room and the rooms beyond. I love to open our windows for fresh air whenever the weather is pleasant.

Indeed, window screens are necessary to keep everything but the fresh air out. But I find these highly functional screens seem to hide the shiny glimmer of the window glass, especially distracting from the "curb appeal" of a home. A friend of mine discovered small screens at a nationwide home supply store that are adjustable and easily removable. They can be slid in the bottom part of your window when you want them and taken out when you don't need them. Now I can let breezes flow when the wind blows and keep my front windows shiny and beautiful in between.

If you have a ceiling or floor fan, turn it on to circulate the air. Take area rugs outside for a good shake to remove dirt, dust, and musty smells. Let them blow in the fresh air. If you live in a damp area prone to mildew and mustiness, a dehumidifier can remove some of the moisture from the air. Changing your home's air filter regularly can clear the air of unhealthy, allergy-aggravating particles that your eyes can't see, but your nose can smell. Houseplants help, too. They not only enhance a living room by cleaning the air of impurities, their greenery is also pleasing to the eye. Nothing beats fresh air for fragrancing our homes!

The Fragrant Fireplace

Pleasant fragrances will bless all who enter for long after the fragrance is gone.

Hearth and home. The two go hand in hand. The smell of a wood-burning fire can lend instant warmth and security to your living room. I can still remember going to visit my grandmother in the winter, and how the cold, clear air invigorated me as I rang her doorbell. But the true pleasure came from going inside. The instant I walked in and smelled the woodsy fragrance of the flaming fire, I felt safe and loved. The memory of that scent still warms me.

If you have a fireplace in your living room, enjoy the wealth of warmth it offers. Use it frequently during the fall and winter months. We have a fire nearly every night we are home in the winter; it takes little effort if you have the right ingredients at hand. Why not prepare for a fire in advance so you can fill your living room with its unmatchable fragrance at the strike of a match?

Several natural ingredients can add fun as well as fragrance to a fire's festivities. Fill a basket with scented pinecones and toss one in occasionally for a sudden burst of scent. In Atlanta, we have pine trees and pinecones galore. I can walk out my back door and collect a basketful of nicely shaped cones, dotting them with a few drops of my favorite essential oil. If you have young children, let them enjoy picking up the pinecones. Whether you purchase them or find and fragrance them yourself, scented pinecones are inexpensive and make a great "hearth-warming" gift.

The heavenly aroma of herbs can fragrance your fire too. Try tying bundles of highly fragrant rosemary or lavender together with twine and tossing a bundle into your fire, alongside the logs.

Beautiful Bouquets

Flowers enhance any room, but especially a living room. It's not just their beauty that captivates, but the incredible, fresh scents many release. If you flip through any home magazine, almost every living room has at least one beautiful bouquet of flowers. Although you can't smell the sweet scent of the flowers through the pages, you would no doubt be drinking in their delectable fragrance if you were sitting in the room.

As you notice the fantastic variety of fragrant flowers God has created, you will be overwhelmed with his creativity. Celebrate this creation by filling a vase with a casual cluster of fragrant flowers and placing it in a prominent spot in your living room. You don't need to be a professional florist to arrange flowers. Let your heart guide you. It's your home, and you are the artist!

When selecting flowers, keep fragrance as well as beauty in mind. Although all fragrant flowers are beautiful, not all beautiful flowers are fragrant. Pick flowers that appeal to your particular sense of smell. White flowers are often the most fragrant and, therefore, most frequently used in perfumes. For highly fragrant bouquets, fill a vase with white blossoms of lilac, lily of the valley, narcissus, gardenia, or tuberose. These flowers have such strong scents that they are most suitable for larger rooms like living rooms. They can also be used in mixed bouquets for smaller rooms. More subtly fragranced flowers, like roses, violets, white carnations, freesia, and hyacinth can enhance your living room or anywhere in your home.

"I am a rose of Sharon, a lily of the valleys."
— Song of Songs 2:1

Pleasing Potpourri

The beauty of flowers is that they can be enjoyed fresh or dried. Unlike fresh flowers, a true potpourri, made from dried flowers and other ingredients and enhanced with rich essential oils, can last for a long time and is relatively inexpensive.

The living room is a wonderful place to scatter bowls of potpourri. Whether it be in a big wooden bowl on a coffee table, or a dainty ceramic dish on a side table, potpourri can be a small gift of scent to the nearby nose. Try placing a basket or bowl of pretty and pleasant-smelling potpourri near the fireplace. The heat of the flames will warm the mixture to release its scent throughout the room. A handful of potpourri thrown directly into the fire can also delight your sense of smell.

The possibilities for containers are as vast as the fragrances available. A peek behind cabinet doors may reveal a treasure tucked away — a piece of pottery, a porcelain tea cup, a crystal bowl, a silver dish, a terra cotta saucer — in which to hold potpourri. I love to fill my beautiful, small, silver and crystal dishes. If you have such lovely containers hiding in your home, bring them out to enjoy, along with their fragrant contents.

Although making your own potpourri is not extremely difficult, a myriad of pleasant-smelling, prepared potpourris are available on the market today. For a long-lasting and pleasing fragrance, be sure to purchase the best quality potpourri you can afford. To assure the highest quality, I recommend purchasing potpourri from specialty shops known for their scents.

Quality potpourris last for years, but their fragrances most likely will not. When needed, revitalize potpourri with a few drops of essential oil. You can also add a seasonal touch to potpourri by enhancing it with a few sprigs of bright red berries and cinnamon pinecones for Christmas or lemon peels and dried yellow rose blossoms for spring.

I recently started a "love bowl" in my living room. Bit by bit, blossom by blossom, I am making my own potpourri. I pluck off loose petals, leaves, and buds from discarded bouquets, dry them, and toss them in the bowl. Some are from flowers I received from those showering me with love. Some are from flowers I bought to fill our home. All are adding to its beauty and fragrance. Consider beginning your own love bowl with your next bouquet of flowers.

Fine Furniture

Caring for fine wood furniture means polishing it regularly to remove inevitable dust and to restore luster. But for me, the true sense of satisfaction I gain from dusting the furniture comes from using a pleasant-smelling polish. I love lemon-scented polish because of its fresh, citrus scent.

You can enhance the lemon fragrance of furniture polish by stashing lemon-scented sachets behind a bookshelf, tying them to a doorknob or the arm of a wooden chair, or stuffing them behind the pillow of a sofa. Making a sachet takes just minutes. Start with a pretty handkerchief or square of decorative fabric. Spoon in a pleas-

"Perfume and incense bring joy to the heart."
— Proverbs 27:9

ing potpourri mixture and tie with a tassel, ribbon, raffia, or twine. For a lemony scent, use a potpourri that contains lemon thyme or lemon verbena. For a twist of freshness, add a few lemon peels.

Delightful Desks

Wherever your work area is, consider making your desk a fragrant place of pleasure. Rub the inside of a desk drawer with a few drops of fragrant essential oil. The wood will slowly absorb and release the oil's scent. Another quick way to make your desk smell pleasant is to place perfumed sachets in desk drawers. A single flower will also enhance your desktop and make any task more tolerable. I love to light a scented candle at my desk while I work and write. The pleasant fragrance that fills the air around me is always an inspiration. When it comes to letter writing, why not share the pleasure fragrance offers and send a scent to someone special by placing a sachet envelope in your stationary box or spraying cologne inside its snug-fitting lid. Let the fragrance penetrate the paper. Next time you dash off a note, both you and the recipient will be blessed by the sweet smell.

For a delightful and easy-to-mail gift, tuck a small sachet envelope in a note to a friend. A dear college friend recently celebrated a birthday in another state. As a fragrant gesture, I laid a sachet envelope of bath crystals in her birthday card and mailed it off. It's the thought that counts, but the fragrance that lasts!

"Little things mean everything."
— Samuel Johnson

Fragrant Kitchens

There is something about an irresistible smell seeping from the kitchen that brings life to any home. Maybe it's the security the smell provides that suggests love and care. Or the comfort it gives hungry appetites knowing they will soon be satisfied. Or maybe it's the curiosity it arouses as the nose tries to identify what's cooking. One thing we do know is that the pleasure we derive from eating comes largely from smell, not simply taste. God intentionally wired these two senses together. Whether it be fresh coffee brewing in the

early morning or cookies baking in the late evening, the smells that fill our kitchens nourish us as much as the foods that fill our stomachs.

What's Cooking?

In her book *Living a Beautiful Life*, Alexandra Stoddard tells of a friend who once told her, "A house becomes a home only when good smells come from the kitchen." And no doubt, those smells are the aromas of delicious foods cooking.

A highlight of my childhood summers was visiting my grandparents for a week. Without fail, I would awake to the homey smell of eggs and bacon frying in the kitchen. Even today when I occasionally inhale the same breakfast aromas, I am reminded of those cozy mornings sitting in their little kitchen in Silver Spring, Maryland, savoring the love and smells showered on me.

"Do everything in love."
— 1 Corinthians 16:14

My grandmother was a good cook. She taught my mother, and my mother passed on to me, the truth that good smells in the kitchen are essential to the enjoyment of your home. "Even if it's just hamburger and onion sautéing in a pan," my mother would tell me, "try to have something cooking when others arrive home for dinner." Why? The smell makes them feel expected; they sense you are anticipating their arrival. It tells people that *their* lives matter enough in *your* life that you would stop other things to prepare food for them.

The encouraging news is that cooking can be simple. A tragedy in many homes today is the lost art of cooking and, therefore, the lost aroma of cooking. People have forgotten that filling their kitchens with good food fragrances need not be a chore — it can be as easy as a pot of soup simmering on the stove, or a roast fresh out of the package, rubbed in butter and garlic, sizzling in the oven. After a busy day, all I need to do to bring fragrance to my kitchen is to have scrubbed potatoes baking in the oven.

The important fact to remember when cooking is that it's the actual cooking process that gives off the strong, enticing smells. That is why reheating a fully cooked food does not release the same potent aroma — the majority of the wonderful, fragrant particles were released while the food was being cooked the first time. Next time you microwave a frozen meal, notice how slight the smell of it cooking is compared to that of microwaving something fresh.

If you are gone during the day, or if you are home and simply desire an easy way to prepare delicious-smelling meals, use a crock pot. A few years back, Bill and I went on vacation with several couples. To lighten the kitchen load for all, each couple was in charge of a meal. While some of us slaved in the kitchen to prepare our meals, my friend Vanessa was smart. In the morning, she smothered a beef brisket with barbecue sauce, wrapped it in foil, and set it in a covered crock-pot. When the women arrived back from a fun day antiquing and the men from playing golf, the delicious aroma of barbecue awaited us. There's nothing like coming home and smelling supper cooking, especially when you are the cook!

Before having guests to our home, I ask myself, "What good scents will they smell when they walk in?" Sometimes during the cold months, the minute I hear the doorbell ring, I push the "start" button on my microwave oven to begin popping popcorn. By the time we've greeted our guests and made our way to the kitchen, the buttery smell steams the air. The gesture seems simple, but the smell is so satisfying. For a spicy-scented warm beverage, simmer cinnamon sticks, cloves, and orange peels in apple juice. If you don't have apple juice on hand, use boiling water. Although you can't drink it, it smells wonderful!

During the warmer months, I use my stove and oven less frequently, and my kitchen is less apt to be filled with the warm, heavy smells of pot roast or spaghetti. So, although many of our meals in the spring and summer are served cold, I make a conscious effort to bake fresh, hot rolls or steam corn on the cob or asparagus in order to enhance the smells in my kitchen.

How is it that a smell so delightful can be so indescribable?

Baked Blessings

The fragrance of bread baking immediately conjures up a sense of coziness and comfort, a feeling of "home." No wonder real estate agents suggest baking bread when prospective buyers are looking at your home — it pulls on people's heartstrings. Our last home sold the second week it was on the market. Certainly, the timing was in God's ultimate control, but the warm bread baking in the oven probably didn't hurt!

You need to know that I am not a bread baker. I don't know if I will ever be. But I recognize the benefits of bread baking enough to find a way to somehow fill my kitchen with its soothing scent. A bread oven is one easy solution that will save your time and your knuckles, but still fill your home and your stomachs with the pleasure of truly homemade bread.

My favorite bread to bake is frozen bread. It's bread baking without the bread making! Frozen yeast rolls or loaves can be purchased in most grocery stores. Let them rise and bake, and your kitchen smells delicious instantly. I learned this at a party at our friends' the McCollum's. They teach a church's engaged couples class and had opened their home for a party. At the time, Bill was an associate pastor, so we were invited. While the kitchen bustled with activity, I commented to Margie on the marvelous smell of the homemade rolls baking. She hesitated to tell me she had used frozen dough for fear the soon-to-be wives might see her as lazy. I laughed and assured her nothing would relieve or inspire them more than knowing her secret. I have since passed on this tip to many who have enjoyed the same delicious-smelling bread in our kitchen.

Certainly, there is no substitute for homemade bread. If you have time and enjoy making it, roll up your sleeves and go for it. But if baking is a burden to you, remember the main purpose of creating a "SenseSational" home is to make where we live a place of pleasure and ministry. It's the smells coming from our kitchens that matter, not how long it takes to make them.

The smell of sweet goodies baking is a fragrance that fills the heart as it fills the kitchen. For a mouthwatering scent, make an easy dessert that can be assembled, but not baked, before a meal. Place it in the oven when you sit down to eat. The delicious smell of dessert baking will tempt your nose just when your sweet tooth's ready.

A marvelous way to scent your kitchen is with cake candles. They smell good enough to eat! I discovered these delicious delights while working at a design shop called Persnickety. I kept one lit at all times while I manned the shop, and the candles sold like crazy. Cake candles are large, 4 x 4, sweet-scented candles that come in kitchen fragrances like cinnamon spice, vanilla, applesauce, cranberry, plum pudding, and chocolate devil's food cake. They last for days and make your home smell like you have been baking for hours. You can find them in many gift and country craft shops. I

"Bread deals with living things, with giving life, with growth, with the seed, the grain that natures."
—Lionel Poilâne

enjoy their scent so much, I not only use them throughout my home, I even keep them on hand for housewarming gifts.

Freshly Brewed

I don't love mornings, but I do love coffee. The first scent of coffee brewing somehow stimulates me to want to wake up. As I inhale this delightful drink directly beneath my nose, I am no longer groggy, but suddenly grateful to begin a new day. If you or those you love drink coffee, let the aroma of it brewing lure you out of bed in the morning or settle you in the evening. With today's coffee makers, it's fairly easy to make coffee the night before and set a timer to turn it on ten minutes before your alarm sounds.

For an occasional treat, I use a coffee grinder to grind fresh, whole, coffee beans and a dash of cinnamon. You can't beat the scent of freshly-ground coffee beans brewing! Many times, if we are expecting guests, Bill prepares the coffee before they arrive. As we are winding down our meal, one of us slips into the kitchen to turn it on. In minutes, the aroma of coffee fills the air.

Fruit-Filled Aromas

The sweet scent of fruit is a natural way to provide fragrance to your kitchen. A bowl of fresh apples on the kitchen table or a strawberry-scented candle burning by the sink can give off a sweet aroma that lures you and others to linger in the kitchen. Sachet envelopes come in fruit fragrances like apples, peaches, and strawberries. I have found that even a full pantry smells "empty" because it tends to store cans and packaged goods, so I have an apple-scented sachet in mine. Why not tuck one on your pantry shelf to tempt your nose?

The zingy zest of citrus can sweeten your kitchen too. I love the cheerful yellow of lemons, so I often cluster an armful of lemons in a majolica bowl in my kitchen. When I notice one is looking old, I cut it in half and grind it in my garbage disposal to replace unpleasant food odors with a lively, lemony scent. Another way to freshen with citrus is to place fresh peelings from a lemon, lime, or orange in a dish in a ventilated area. It will quickly freshen your kitchen air.

"Smell is the mute sense, the one without words."
— Diane Ackerman

Heavenly-Scented Flowers and Herbs

The aroma of flowers and herbs can also enhance the pleasure of your kitchen. A casual cluster of fresh-cut flowers by your kitchen sink provides a friendly fragrance as you cook and clean up. Place them in an informal kitchen container like a pitcher or a teapot. Try to place flowers in a spot that will be in view and a whiff away, but not in the way.

"The smell of basil is good—for the heart and the head . . ."
—John Gerard

I enjoy taking a simple mason jar tied with a raffia bow, filling it with a handful of sweet-smelling daffodils from my backyard, and setting it on the ledge above my sink. The arrangement looks effortless, and the blossoms smell wonderful. Terra cotta pots of fragrant planted flowers can also perfume your kitchen, and will last longer than fresh-cut flowers.

Herbs, as well as flowers, make fragrant bouquets. The advantage of herbs in the kitchen is that, in addition to lending a sweetness to the air we breathe, they add a hint of flavor to the food we eat. Buy a bouquet of fragrant, fresh herbs like lemon thyme, mint, rosemary, parsley, sage, tarragon, or sweet basil. Whether you display it in a pitcher, hang it from a pantry door, or lay it in a basket, your herb bouquet will lend a healthy aroma to your kitchen and be just an arm's length away for cooking. Consider taking along an herb bouquet when visiting a friend. Wrap it in brown paper and tie it with twine for an all-natural look.

My friend Lauren Salter brought me a mint bouquet with roots intact fresh out of her garden. I was touched by such a thoughtful gift of love and life. It took just a few minutes to plant the roots in a sunny spot in our backyard, and the mint seemed to grow overnight. Now we enjoy the sweet scent of mint in our own home and share it with others.

Herbs can also be purchased as wreaths or topiaries and make delightfully-scented decorations for any kitchen. A friend of mine has a bay leaf wreath that adorns her kitchen wall and welcomes others with its beauty and fragrance.

Freshen Up

Foods that smelled pleasant while cooking may not seem so if their aromas linger. Freshening up your kitchen can help eliminate the unpleasant odors often found here. Unscented candles and sprays that remove or neutralize odors are perfect for the kitchen, clearing the air so more pleasant fragrances can be enjoyed.

Opening the refrigerator door can be refreshing or revolting, as refrigerators tend to absorb the aromas of the foods with which we fill them. The scents, pleasant or unpleasant, coming from your refrigerator may actually affect how you feel about food preparation. Before going shopping to the grocery store, I throw away any spoiled items and wipe out my refrigerator and freezer with a mild, fragrant soap and warm water. When I return with fresh food, it is a joy to stock the clean, sweet-smelling refrigerator. Add a box of baking soda to your refrigerator and freezer to absorb strong odors (try a box with spill-proof vents).

The kitchen trash can is an obvious place for unpleasant aromas. With as many times as we open and close it each day, it helps to make the experience as pleasant as possible. I lay a sachet envelope on the bottom of my kitchen trash can under the plastic liner. Try a sachet yourself or take advantage of one of the many other scented products available today, such as scented trash can liners, scented disks that hang or stick to the inside of your can, scented sprays, or a simple sprinkle of baking soda.

"Rose is a rose is a rose is a rose."
— Gertrude Stein

FRAGRANT DINING ROOMS

Dining rooms present a wonderful invitation for fragrance. It is in your dining room that you have a captive audience. While your friends and family eat, drink, and take in the delicious-smelling delicacies prepared in the kitchen, surprise them with other sweet scents scattered about. Keep in mind, the fragrances that fill your dining room should enhance, not distract from the meal. Make sure they don't overpower the appetizing aromas of the food itself.

Whether your dining room is elegant and sophisticated, casual and comfortable, or like ours, casually elegant, you can fragrance it in many ways; however, only a few scents are needed to make your dining room delightful.

The Scented Centerpiece

Perhaps the most obvious place to begin is the center of the dining room table. Not only is it the most vacant surface for display, it is a fragrant focal point noticed by every nose. When selecting scented flowers for your centerpiece, choose those with a soft and gentle perfume — roses, geraniums, and jonquils work beautifully. If you use candles on your dining table, the warmth from the flame will intensify the flowers' fragrance.

Although I like things to be lovely and satisfying, simplicity is the most important quality for me. Because of this, I tend to stick to one type of fragrant flower at a time for most of my centerpieces. I may choose something as casual as geraniums blossoming in a basket or as sophisticated as several white roses in a cut-crystal vase. Either way, the arrangements are pleasing, but not overpowering or overcomplicated.

For a bit of originality and lightheartedness, consider creating a floating scented centerpiece in your dining room. Fill a large, clear glass bowl with scented candles that float, adding in several rose petals. Place the bowl on a pretty tray and surround it with fresh flowers and greens. The glimmer of glowing candles will reflect off the glass and swim throughout the room.

Dried floral arrangements or wreaths are lovely and long-lasting for the center of your dining table. To make them fragrant, add a touch of essential oil to their leaves or use scented potpourri as the base of the arrangement.

"Think big thoughts but relish small pleasures."
— H. Jackson Brown Jr.

Perfumed Place Settings

I see each person God brings to sit at my dining table as someone special. To remind me and them of this, I love to make each setting a place of beauty and fragrance. We have such a short time to sit and share life, why not make the moments at your table as pleasant and memorable as possible? Because of fragrance's powerful influence on memory, perfuming each place setting can enhance the dining experience long after the dishes are done and the lights are dimmed.

Scented votive candles are one of my favorite ways to fragrance each place setting. I stock up on them when I see a sale and store them in my refrigerator (they will burn slower if they are cold) or in my candle drawer. I often place them in pretty stemmed glassware that I seldom otherwise use — the glassware heightens the enjoyment by bringing the candle's fragrance closer to each nose. Clear or colored glass votive candleholders are unobtrusive and work well, too. For a casual look, use miniature terra cotta pots for votive candleholders. Spray or sponge paint them if you want them to coordinate with the colors of your dining room or dinnerware.

A fragrant flower blossom is another simple way to perfume each place setting in your dining room. Individual vases can display scent-filled buds. Just as each guest at your table is unique, collect small, interesting bottles and mix and match them.

For a dinner party of twelve, a dozen roses can bring delightful dividends if you spread their wealth and fragrance to each setting. Tie each long-stem rose with a pretty ribbon and lay it in front of a plate. Consider adding an extra touch by tying a handwritten place card to each ribboned rose. Guests will enjoy the rose's scent while they sit and it will remind them of their dining experience when they've gone home.

Napkins, place mats, and tablecloths can add to your dining table all the more if they are perfumed. The easiest way to do this is to place scented sachets in the drawers that store them.

Napkins are perhaps the most important linen to fragrance, as guests take in their scent each time they wipe their mouths. You can also tie a sachet to each napkin and offer the sachets to your guests as favors they can take with them to fragrance their own homes. When setting your table, spray the underside of each napkin with a light mist of fragrance before pulling it through the napkin ring. Or, if napkins require ironing, iron them with scented spray starch or lightly spray your ironing board with perfume before ironing each one.

Miniature tussie-mussies, small nosegays of flowers and herbs, are wonderful and can be used to enhance each place setting or as garnishes for desserts. In past centuries, particular flowers in tussie-mussies conveyed special messages. Though they are no longer used for that purpose, tussie-mussies still carry scent and sentiment to those who receive them today. To make a simple tussie-mussie, gather a small cluster of fragrant flowers and fresh greens. Add a few sweet-smelling herbs and thread the stems through the center of a small paper doily. Twist the underside of the doily around the stems and wrap it with floral tape. Tie it all together with a pretty bow, and these little bouquets can brighten and perfume every place setting at your table.

If all of these ideas intrigue you, but your guests are arriving any minute, rub a few drops of fragrant essential oil underneath your dining table. The fragranced wood will perfume the room and give off an equally inviting smell. Most of all, remember, the purpose of fragrancing your dining room is to *enhance* the eating experience. Be sure to keep the majority of your table free for food.

"For the sense of smell, almost more than any other, has the power to recall memories and it is a pity that we use it so little."
— Rachel Carson

Blossoming Plants

The dining room is often one of the least furnished rooms in our homes. Why not warm the room with the fragrance and beauty of a sweet-smelling indoor plant? One clear-cut advantage of having a plant with fragrant blooms instead of a vase of fresh-cut flowers is that plants last longer! If your dining room has a sunny spot, consider dwarf variations of lemon or orange citrus trees. Their broad leaves often produce fragrant white flowers in addition to small, citrus-scented fruits.

My favorite blossoming plant is the gardenia bush. To me, their smell is marvelous and memorable. Long ago, my mother's only gift request for a particular Mother's Day was a gardenia bush. The bush filled her heart and home with its lovely fragrance for years. When it finally grew too large to be indoors, my mother repotted it and placed it outdoors. At our wedding, I chose to carry a full bouquet of beautiful gardenias because of their sentimental fragrance. Though my father ushered me down the aisle, the scent of my bouquet wouldn't let me forget my precious mother seated in the front pew. To this day, I love the sweet scent a gardenia gives. Check with your local garden shop for suggestions on fragrant indoor plants that might grow well in your dining room's setting.

FRAGRANT BEDROOMS

Pleasant scents can put even the most weary bodies and souls into a wonderful state of mind. Bedrooms need to be peaceful and soothing sanctuaries, and satisfying smells play a potent part in accomplishing this purpose. Sweet, sensual, and subtle fragrances should lure you and those you love into this most replenishing room in your home.

Sweet-Smelling Dreams

The bed is a wonderful place to allow fragrance to blossom. Beds have long been a place to store aromas. Centuries before the creation of spring mattresses, beds were filled with fragrant grasses and mattresses were stuffed with rose petals. Although neither probably proved extremely comfortable, I'm sure they smelled delightful.

Fortunately, enhancing a bed's fragrance today is a much easier task. First, think about your sheets. How pleasant-smelling are they at this very moment? You may not enjoy changing your sheets, but isn't it wonderful to crawl into them the first night after they have been laundered? Change your sheets as frequently as possible, laundering them with a perfumed detergent pleasing to you and to those you love. Between washings, air your sheets out and fragrance them lightly with a pleasant perfume. On a warm summer night, turn down your sheets and sprinkle them with a fragrant body talc before you turn in. This perfumed powder absorbs moisture, so it will delight your nose *and* keep your body dry. When storing bed linens, tuck a soothing sachet or a few sprigs of lavender in between them. Lavender is a lovely, natural way to fragrance your linen closet. Its luscious scent also repels moths, fleas, silverfish, and flies.

A pillow filled with herbs and flowers was once thought to induce sleep and even prevent bad dreams. King George III of England insisted he could not sleep without his hops-stuffed pillow! While their sleeping effects may be debatable, the scents of fresh herbs and spices such as vanilla and chamomile are still believed to soothe and relax. For a sweet treat, slip a scented rosemary, lemon, or rose sachet in your pillowcase or sham. Pinning a decorative fabric sachet to the outside of a pretty pillow can also perfume your bed.

Bedside tables, large or small, skirted or bare wood, are a perfect spot to rest a touch of fragrance. A single bud or a bouquet bursting with blossoms serves the same purpose: You will drift off to sleep by its sweet smell and wake up to a wonderful whiff of it. Try subtle fragrances like freesia, roses, or a single stem of a pink-and-white stargazer lily on your night stand. When purchasing flowers, select those that have several closed buds. The flowers will last longer, gradually opening over several days and slowly releasing their delicate scent.

"I have perfumed my bed with myrrh, aloes and cinnamon."
— Proverbs 7:17

If you are married, don't forget to place fragrant flowers on both sides of your bed. I enjoy buying a bouquet of flowers, dividing them up, and scattering their beauty and scent around the bedroom. One bouquet can go a long way! You can also add fragrance beside your bed with a scented candle, a lamp ring with essential oil, or a spray of perfume on a cool bulb before turning a lamp on low. I use a scented ring on a lamp beside our bed and enjoy changing its fragrances frequently.

Because space to display fragrance in a bedroom is limited, suspending scented decorations is a pleasant solution. If you have a poster bed, consider hanging a bouquet of softly-scented fresh flowers or colorful dried flowers dotted with essential oil. Decorative sachets hanging from doorknobs or furniture hardware can also add to the scented spirit of your bedroom.

The Delightful Dresser

Dressers can be scented beautifully inside and out. If room allows, fragrant flowers can enhance the top of a dresser — especially in front of a mirror, where the reflection will multiply their beauty. A pretty bowl of potpourri can perfectly perfume the corner of a dresser of any kind.

There are many ways to bring fragrance inside dresser drawers. I often lay an almost-empty bottle of perfume in my lingerie drawer where the evaporating perfume can permeate my intimate apparel, leaving a lovely scent. And a dab of essential oil to the dresser back or drawers adds a quick touch of fragrance as it is absorbed by the wood.

To effortlessly fragrance dresser drawers, take advantage of wonderful sachet envelopes available in every scent imaginable. Stash one in every dresser drawer — but don't save all the scent for yourself! Surprise your husband, children, or guests with a lovely, sachet envelope to fragrance their drawers as well. They are relatively inexpensive and take no more effort than to buy and try. Most men prefer spicy scents, and young children tend to like fruit scents. Spoil them with a drawer full of satisfying smells.

Splurge on scent by lining your drawers with pretty, perfumed drawer liners. Select decorative papers that both look and smell lovely in your bedroom. True, it may take a few minutes of effort to cut them to size and rubber cement them in, but as you empty your drawers to line them, you may be inspired to tidy things up. You will be doubly blessed with fragrant and orderly drawers. Though fragrances used in enclosed areas like dresser drawers do last longer than those in open air, the scent of drawer liners won't last forever. To replenish them, simply spray several squirts of perfume on the paper.

A Closet of Scent

Even in Old Testament days, fragrant clothing was satisfying. One psalmist, writing a wedding song for the royal king, notices, "All your robes are fragrant with myrrh and aloes and cassia" (Psalm 45:8). In Song of Songs, the beloved groom admires the scent of his bride's perfumed clothes, chanting, "The fragrance of your garments is like that of Lebanon" (Song of Songs 4:11). Fragrant garments suggested celebration and brought immense pleasure. Today, they still can.

Unfortunately, the closets that store our clothes are prone to be places that also store unpleasant smells. Although soiled laundry and sweaty shoes are unavoidable, little things can make our clothes closet more agreeable. Cedar and lavender are the most suitable scents for closets that store clothing; their natural fragrances are pleasant and protect clothing from pests like moths and silverfish. Consider using cedar shoe trees to keep your shoes and

"All your robes are fragrant of myrrh and aloes and cassia."
—Psalms 45:8

your closet smelling forest-fresh. Bill uses cedar shoe trees, and I use plastic shoe trees and then store each pair of shoes in a clear, plastic box with a scented sachet envelope. Both methods keep our feet smelling sweet and our shoes in tip-top shape. For athletic footwear or feet that perspire profusely, occasionally sprinkle fragrant powder in shoes.

When you lift the lid to your hamper, how bad is the smell? Most of us don't wash laundry every day, so in the meantime, anything we can do to control the odor from soiled clothing helps. Try placing a box of baking soda with a spill-proof vent in the bottom of your clothes hamper to reduce dirty laundry odor.

Cedar hangers or scented padded hangers add a pleasant fragrance to your nicer garments. All of Bill's blazers and suits hang on cedar hangers. I like to use scented padded hangers to hang jackets and special dresses; they seem more feminine. Their padding prevents hanger bulges in clothing sleeves, and their scent makes getting dressed a pleasure.

Have fun scenting and storing your clothing as you anticipate a change of season. Like a squirrel that stashes away nuts to savor for a later time, stow away surprises like scented soaps, bundles of lavender, or cedar blocks. Stash them wherever you store your clothing: cedar or blanket chests, zippered hanging wardrobes, or clear, plastic bags and cardboard boxes. I don't personally care for the pungent aroma of mothballs. Although their fragrance carries fond memories of my Grandmother Ryan's home, I find cedar to be a more subtle and soothing alternative. Suit your nose as you store your clothes.

A Passion for Perfume

Some, perhaps, may view perfume as a luxury; but to me, its feminine fragrance on my skin causes me to celebrate being a lady. And that is well worth its price! Like jewelry, personal fragrance is a beauty accessory — it is the finishing touch to who I am on the outside and a refreshing reminder of who I represent on the inside. I always spray on a perfume that most suits my attitude and my attire for that day.

When I was first married, a dear friend and spiritual mentor, Patti Tattersal, gave me a lovely crystal perfume bottle with a note

"Pleasing is the fragrance of your perfumes."
— Song of Songs 1:3

attached quoting 2 Corinthians 2:14: "But thanks be to God, who always leads us in triumphal procession in Christ and through us spreads everywhere the fragrance of the knowledge of him." Her words encouraged me to use my life to spread the "sweet aroma" of Christ. I was touched by her thoughtful and challenging reminder of my purpose here on earth. That precious perfume bottle is now filled with a sweet aroma of its own and has adorned my dresser for years.

Personal fragrances are equally satisfying for men. Bill has several colognes displayed on his mahogany chest of drawers. Each scent represents sentimental seasons in our life together. Lagerfield, for instance, conjures up memories of our dating. To this day, when he splashes some on, I immediately become a twenty-five-year-old girl excited to hold my young love's hand.

Because many fragrances are expensive, you will want them to last as long as possible, both in the bottle and on your body. When displaying fragrances on your dresser, keep them at room temperature and away from bright light. When wearing fragrance, apply it to your pulse points: behind your ears, at your throat, between your breasts, inside your wrists, or behind your knees. The warmth and vibration of your skin in these spots will gently release the fragrance.

FRAGRANT BATHROOMS

Bathrooms are our most private and personal places to perfume. Here, we refresh and rejuvenate ourselves for a new day and we wash ourselves as the day winds down. A little fragrant pampering in the bathroom can greatly affect our perspective on life beyond it. To make our bathroom experience delightful, we need to scent the air and our bodies with fabulous fragrances.

Perfume the Air

The purpose for perfuming the bathroom is twofold: to mask or remove unfavorable odors and to add pleasant ones. You can fragrance the air in your bathrooms or powder room in a variety of ways. Although these rooms are proportionately smaller than most other rooms in the home, the scents used to fragrance a bathroom may be strong. Few fragrances will overwhelm you during the small amount of time you are in the bathroom.

Scented room sprays are a safe and simple way to fragrance your bathroom. I keep a can of scented room spray visible in every bathroom of our home in a place convenient for family and friends to use. There are a vast variety of scented sprays available today. Select one you enjoy. I celebrate the seasons in my bathrooms by changing the scent of my bathroom spray. You may find the scent of gardenia in the spring, cinnamon spice in the fall, or pine in the winter.

Scented sprays are lovely, but they don't last long. Consider enhancing their fragrance with a burning candle of the same or complementary scent. The gesture of a scented candle in a powder room is not only fragrant, but welcoming. I remember having lunch years ago at my friend Cindy Kusmer's home. I was her only guest. When I walked into her powder room, I saw that she had lit a beautiful scented candle. I was touched by her thoughtfulness just for me!

I love to light a scented candle by my bathtub and keep the lights dim when I'm soaking in the warm water. I have even been known to light a scented candle for a special bath time at Aunt T's with my niece and nephew, Katy and Van. They love it! We're never too young to enjoy the simple scented pleasures God has given us in life.

If you have a scented candle in your bathroom (and you don't have young children), leave a pretty book of matches beside the candle. Not only will it invite anyone to light the candle at the strike of a match, but the simple smell of a burnt match will instantly override adverse aromas and neutralize the bathroom's fragrance. I have a friend who carries a book of matches for this very purpose when she travels. If you choose to spray air freshener after lighting a match, a light spray will be all you will need.

You need only to walk the cleaning products aisle of most grocery stores to be amazed by the mass of fragrant products available to scent your bathroom. Look them over. Take a sniff. There are fragrances to hang in the toilet, plug into an electrical outlet, or simply sit on a counter. I personally prefer more decorative and natural

"And the house was filled with the fragrance of the perfume."
—John 12:13

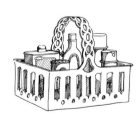

fragrances than these, but the most important thing is to choose a scent and product that appeals to your sense of smell and your lifestyle.

Aromatic Accessories

Given the proper conditions, fragrant flowers and plants can bring life to an otherwise seemingly sterile bathroom. In addition to the beauty and scent they lend to the bathroom, fragrant flowers and plants benefit from the room's warmth and humidity. Place a single blossom or petite bouquet of flowers by your sink, behind the toilet, or in any nook looking for a touch of fragrant charm. Add a few sprigs of mint for refreshing, scented greenery. Terra cotta pots of flowering plants, like geraniums, can line a sunny window ledge or sit on the bathroom floor. Or, if your bathroom has a skylight or large window, hang a flowering jasmine overhead to shower you with its sweet scent. I like to collect small vases and cluster several together on my bathroom countertop. Each one may hold only a few buds, but together they create a miniature masterpiece.

After a long day, if you want to clear the air and your head, eucalyptus may be just what the doctor ordered. Eucalyptus is among the most aromatic plants in the world and has been widely used to treat respiratory conditions for centuries. For a fragrant treat, tie a bouquet or wreath of eucalyptus to your showerhead with a few strands of raffia. The warm, moist steam from a hot shower will release the eucalyptus' cool and invigorating scent. The smell of eucalyptus carries me back to my childhood. When I had a cold, my mother would massage a greasy, menthol-scented rub on my chest and turn on the steamy vaporizer. The combination of her soothing touch, the hypnotizing hum of the vaporizer, and the cool smell of eucalyptus always made me feel better.

Scented seashells are a beautiful and interesting way to fragrance a bathroom. They give a touch of the seashore to your own little ocean — your bathtub. You'll find scented seashells in many gift shops. Or, to scent personal treasures you collected while walking sandy shores, soak small shells in an essential oil. For larger shells, like conch shells, simply dot a few drops of fragrant oil in their centers. Unlike fragile potpourri that will wither in the bathroom's moist environment, the seashell is a perfect vessel to perfume. If you live near the beach or simply love the beauty, texture, and shapes of seashells, as I do, consider adorning your bathroom shelves with a few fragrant seashells.

Your Body

For a crash course in the satisfaction a scented body can bring, skim through Song of Songs. The pleasure of fragrancing our bodies has long been known; it's the frequency and ease with which we do it that has changed. The most difficult part of perfuming our bodies today is choosing from the millions of products on the market! Our bathrooms are the place we stash these treasures of scented beauty products.

"The fragrance of your breath [is] like apples."
— Song of Songs 7:8

Skin is obviously the largest source of personal odor, and keeping it clean and fragrant requires more than rinsing with water. Scented lotions, cleansers, deodorants, powders, even scented tissue and toilet paper, all provide fragrance to the skin. Many perfume manufacturers make different products like powders, lotions, and perfumes all with the same scent. Be selective; the more products you use of the same scent to fragrance your body, the more enticing the smell will be. I discovered this recently with a delightful perfume. I loved the sweet, floral fragrance, but it didn't seem to last on my skin. On a later trip to the store, a salesperson suggested I try wearing a body lotion with the same scent. The two together enhance the scent, and the wonderful fragrance lasts a long time.

Scented soaps can fragrance our bodies and enhance our bath or shower experience. I still enjoy the clean, innocent smell of Ivory soap. As a young girl, I lathered with this soap in the showers of our local pool, and today I keep liquid Ivory beside the sinks in my home. The smell of my Ivory-clean hands never ceases to make me feel young again.

Scented soaps come in all sizes, shapes, and fragrances. Fill a pretty dish in your powder room with several, small scented soaps. I have tiny scented bunny rabbit and heart soaps in our guest bathroom. Little children who come to our home insist on washing their hands frequently, and I think these fun, fragrant soaps have something to do with it! Let those you love and live with pick the soap that pleases them the most. Who knows what memories you might be making?

Many body soaps are now not only scented, but deodorizing as well. Before going into ministry, Bill worked for Procter & Gamble. He was a loyal employee then and remains loyal to their fine products today. The soap dish in our shower always holds a white bar of Safeguard. It satisfies our sense of smell and cleans and deodorizes our bodies, all at the same time.

I am especially particular about the smell of my hair-care products. After all, the hair on my head frames my face, which houses my nose. It's close by! When narrowing down my shampoo choices, I base my decision first on its qualities, second on its price, and the tie breaker is usually the one that smells best. The aromas of extinct shampoos like Lemon Up, Herbal Essence, and Gee . . . Your Hair Smells Terrific remind me of my teen years. What are your favorite fragranced hair products?

A perfumed bath or shower is a luxurious way to pamper yourself in the privacy of your bathroom. The bathing experience is more popular than ever. As a result, ingredients to fragrance our bodies and bath water abound: salts, oils, crystals, gels, grains, beads, and bubbles. Make a date to draw up a hot bath for yourself. Slow down and soak in a tubful of scented warm water. Savor the smell as you close your eyes and thank God for the many blessings in your life.

Tiny Thought

Lord,
Fill my home with your fragrance
Of love both good and sweet,
So it will give a breath of freshness
To everyone I greet.

Tips for Fragrancing Your Home

Light up your life. Light a scented candle when you spend time with God. The fragrant smell will calm your spirits, bringing you pleasure and peace while you focus on him.

Mark the spot with scent. Use a small sachet envelope as a scented bookmark in your Bible or the latest literature beside your bed. The fragrance will make reading so enjoyable you won't want to put the book down!

Celebrate your femininity. Use a lovely, tasseled perfume atomizer to spray on a light mist of your favorite fragrance. It's a luxury that will make you feel like a lady!

Be my guest. What's more welcoming than a wonderful fragrance? Greet guests to your home with fragrant flowers by their bed and a small gift basket filled with perfumed products to scent their bodies.

Pack a perfume. Store sachets in unused luggage. Next time your travel, keep the sachet in your suitcase to keep it smelling fresh.

Give it away! When wrapping gifts, top them off with a touch of fragrance. Tie a rose, sachet, or cinnamon stick in the bow.

Become "scentimental." Open your eyes and your nose to the bouquet of fragrances around you. When you smell a pleasant scent, close your eyes and enjoy it. Make a mental note of the wonderful scent. Thank God for it.

Live it up! Extend the life and fragrance of your fresh flowers by adding a little chlorine bleach and sugar to lukewarm water. Trim the flower stems and change water daily.

Lather in loveliness. Before crawling into bed at night, clean your body with a quick, hot shower or a long, warm bath. Top yourself off with a sprinkle of favorite-smelling bath powder.

Chapter Four

~

Tantalizing the
Taste Buds

For he satisfies the thirsty and fills the
hungry with good things.
Psalm 107:9

A Taste of Taste

I love going to our local farmers' market. The minute I walk through the door, I am surrounded by the bustling sound of activity like bees swarming around a honeycomb. I love smelling bread baking, coffee brewing, and flowers bursting with fragrance. I love taking in every color and texture and shape of fruits and vegetables imaginable as I reach out to touch an avocado for ripeness or loaf of bread for softness.

But perhaps the most alluring part of going to the market is that, all along the way, my taste buds are tantalized with samples: slices of tart and sweet apples, wedges of sweet melons, sips of rich cider and fresh-squeezed orange juice, and nibbles of warm cinnamon bread. It's a Disneyland for the taste buds! Wandering through the wonderful aisles, I am amazed at the abundant bounty of delicious foods and beverages God has given us to enjoy.

We each have approximately ten thousand tiny taste buds with which to take in the flavors of foods God created. Yet, the satisfaction we get from tasting something requires more than our taste buds, for the sense of taste is largely dependent on our other senses. In fact, taste is the only sense that is impossible to experience without stimulating at least one of the other senses first.

The sense that taste is most closely linked to is our sense of smell. While God has wired up our noses to detect endless odors, the taste buds on our tongues can identify only sweet, salty, bitter, and sour tastes. Therefore, much of the pleasure derived from eating actually comes from smelling what we eat. First we see and smell the food before us, then we touch the food or drink to our tongue, and finally, we taste it.

Taste Energizes

Eating the proper foods provides us with the energy we need to live. Just as an automobile needs refueling to run, our bodies must

"They will rejoice in the bounty of the Lord . . ."
— Jeremiah 31:12

have a continuous supply of the right foods — especially carbohydrates — to have energy to function. Everything we do uses energy: running, walking, talking, writing, even sleeping. Energy powers our hearts to beat, our lungs to breathe, and our brains to think.

Filled with stored-up energy from the sun, plant foods provide our bodies with simple carbohydrates or instant energy. Found in fresh fruits and non-starchy vegetables, these energy-giving carbohydrates are full of vitamins, minerals, and fiber that, once digested, can be quickly released into our systems to give us energy to burn.

Complex carbohydrates take longer to convert into energy, but they also benefit our bodies. The evening before a marathon, runners will load up on complex carbohydrates like pasta, rice, or potatoes. As they run the race, these carbohydrates slowly release into their bodies to give them the energy their body needs. Filling our homes with fresh fruits, vegetables, and pastas will ensure that our bodies have the strength and energy we need to live life to the fullest.

Taste Sustains

Taste also sustains and nourishes our bodies. So our bodies would grow and heal properly, God designed them to require certain nutrients in food. Animal foods are our greatest source of body-building proteins, and fresh foods like seafood, poultry, lean meats, cheeses, and milk all contain protein our bodies need. They help boost the body's metabolism, build muscles, heal and fight infections, and make skin, hair, and nails beautiful and strong. All these body-building nutrients affect how we look and feel, and how we look and feel certainly affects our home life.

Taste Satisfies

Imagine how dull life would be if all God had created for us to eat was a tasteless diet of oatmeal. Even if it strengthened and sustained us, we would miss out on one of the greatest benefits food brings: different, delicious, satisfying tastes. Each different taste gives us the chance to appreciate something delectable.

I love to watch my brother-in-law Ernie eat. When he tastes something wonderful, he closes his eyes in concentration and gently taps his tongue to the roof of his mouth, relishing the pure pleasure and simple satisfaction of eating. What a blessing we miss when we fail to slow down and savor the flavors God has created.

The pleasure taste brings to the home is largely in our control. We have the freedom to choose which foods we will have in our homes, how we will prepare and serve the foods, and when and where we will eat them. We have the opportunity to fill our homes with life and love by filling them with God's delicious bounty. As we do, our family and friends will be richly satisfied.

Taste Today

In today's society, as life bustles with busyness, food preparation and the mealtime ritual have become less and less a part of home life. Many meals are eaten on the run, out of a wrapper, or behind the wheel. And, in an effort to "improve" foods to look prettier, last longer, and taste better, manufacturers have stripped the life-giving nutrients from foods through processing. Many of the foods that line our grocery store shelves are processed. Though this kind of food may bring short-term satisfaction to our taste buds, it distorts our diet and deviates from the natural, nutrient-filled foods God created and intended for our bodies.

Eating well today requires that we select foods that appeal not only to our taste buds, but also to the health and well-being of our bodies. The good news is that God is still in the food business, and he continues to provide food that is delicious, nutritious, and natural. The more we fill our homes and bodies with these kinds of foods, the fuller and healthier lives we will lead.

More and more manufacturers are recognizing the need to offer healthful foods that are also convenient. Many television channels offer a variety of cooking shows to teach healthy, easy food preparation. Tantalizing your family's taste buds with healthy food and drink can be quick and easy with the abundance of fresh-squeezed juices, whole-grain breads, prewashed salad greens, and many other all-natural foods on the market.

"Everything is permissable' — but not everything is beneficial."
— 1 Corinthians 10:23

— ⚜ —

TANTALIZING EXTERIORS

My favorite place to eat is the outdoors. Surrounded by the magnificent sights, sounds, and smells of nature, I somehow feel closer to the Creator of the food I am enjoying. Whether it be a porch off your apartment, a patio or deck behind your house, or a blanket in your backyard, take advantage of every possible opportunity to make mealtimes magical by dining outdoors.

On an early morning when spring is in the air, serve a leisurely weekend breakfast outside or sit and sip a cup of tea while you spend time alone with God. On a clear, sunny afternoon, eat lunch in your bathing suit while you and your family work in the yard, play in the sprinkler, or bask in the warm sun. On a calm, cool evening, sit outside before dinner and enjoy a beverage and appetizer as you wind down the day. Or better still, dine by candlelight under the stars. You have little more to do than prepare the meal — God has already set the stage.

The Great Taste of Grilling

Whether with gas or charcoal, outdoor grilling is a superb cooking method. Not only does it lend a delicious flavor to your food, it's easy — and cleanup is a cinch! When we eat at home during the spring and summer, most of our dinners are either served cold or cooked on the grill. Even in the crisp, cool fall months, we use the grill for tasty meals.

When we talk of grilling, we often think of barbecuing steaks, burgers, or hot dogs. But why not break out of the mold and grill something new, like a healthy piece of salmon or tuna marinated in lime juice and teriyaki sauce or chicken marinated in Dijon mustard or soy sauce? Or tenderize a flank steak in Italian dressing or grill swordfish, amberjack, or grouper in butter, lemon juice, and spices. Use a basket grill to secure and flip food you are grilling, or lay a piece of heavy-duty foil on your grill for fragile foods, like fish.

Many vegetables taste delicious grilled. Try covering corn on the cob, squash, whole onions, or baked or new potatoes, with butter, salt, and pepper wrapped in heavy-duty foil and toss them on your grill. Grilling vegetables also saves dirty dishes and allows you to be outside enjoying family, friends, and fresh air.

For a great meal on the grill, combine meat and vegetables and make shish kebabs. Simply alternate fresh meat and vegetables on a long metal skewer. Try shrimp, boneless chicken, or beef, with fresh vegetables like cherry tomatoes, whole mushrooms, quartered onions, and green pepper chunks. Serve them with whole-grain brown rice and a green salad with fresh fruit. Shish kebabs are a wonderful make-ahead meal to serve guests. The menu will be simple, delicious, and healthy, the presentation colorful.

"Close to nature is close to perfect."
— Pepperidge Farms

Outdoors is the ideal casual setting to enjoy the tasty pleasure of finger foods. Whether it's barbecue chicken or ribs hot off the grill, or crab, shrimp, or corn fresh from the steam pot, all invite you to roll up your sleeves and dig in. Finger foods add to fun outdoor festivities. I enjoy serving foods that you can use your fingers to eat because they make great memory meals. The more senses you use when eating, the more you will retain the experience.

Several years ago, we had a "shrimp peel" in our backyard for some of the leadership at our church. We set up long tables covered in paper tablecloths and let guests finger their way through a feast of all the fresh "peel and eat" shrimp and buttery corn on the cob they could eat. We topped off the meal with chunks of sweet watermelon. It was a messy, but unforgettable time of fun with friends we've grown to love.

An all-time favorite outdoor dessert is s'mores. Made of graham crackers, chocolate bars, and roasted marshmallows, a mouthful of this marvelous, layered luxury takes me back to summer vacations and bonfires on the beaches of Kitty Hawk, North Carolina. Why save such a fun dessert for vacations or campfires? For an easy, no-fuss dessert and occasional sweet splurge, let everyone roast their own marshmallows over the backyard grill and make s'mores.

A Sweet Sip Outdoors

Living in the south, people drink a great deal of iced tea year-round. Most prefer what is called "sweet tea," iced tea already sweetened with sugar. Whether you like your iced tea sweetened or unsweetened, a glass jar of fresh water, a few bags of tea (I use decaffeinated), and the warm sunshine God has given are all the ingredients needed to make delicious sun tea outdoors. Just let the loosely-lidded jar of water and tea steep in the sun for a few hours, stir in some sugar, and refrigerate. If the sun is shining, I'll make a fresh pitcher of sun tea on the table of my back patio every few days. Nature brews it, and I serve it. It's so simple, but so satisfying!

"She opens her arms to the poor and extends her hands to the needy."
— Proverbs 31:20

If you have young children, a fun way to teach them to enjoy serving others is to have an outdoor lemonade stand. As a little girl, my sister and I loved setting up a lemonade stand at the bottom of our grandmother's hill beside her mailbox. We would serve refreshments to the passing neighbors and smile when we saw their satisfaction at having their thirst quenched. Though much time has passed since then, the memory lives on. I even occasionally help my niece and nephew set up a similar lemonade stand on a corner outside their home in our neighborhood. As I sit close by and watch, they learn to put ice in cups, pour and serve the lemonade, and say "Thank you" and "Have a nice day." We don't charge for the lemonade; the experience is priceless. Instead, we just enjoy the outdoors, visit with neighbors, and sip on a few tasty, cold glasses of our own.

Fresh From Your Own Backyard

Growing fresh fruit or vegetables in your own garden is a wonderful way to tantalize your taste buds. Some of the hardiest and easiest-to-grow vegetables are tomatoes, lettuce, cucumbers, summer squash, beets, and radishes. If you have a small, sunny spot in your backyard and the slightest urge to grow something, why not try one little tomato and see what happens? What do you have to lose? A little time, sunshine, and water may breed tasty rewards.

I have never grown my own fresh fruits and vegetables, nor do I foresee I will, as long as I live in a large city like Atlanta where I am blessed to have delicious produce available close by. But I do grow fresh mint and love to use it to enhance iced tea, salads, or small flower arrangements. I hope to begin an herb garden outside my kitchen door soon, filled with parsley, basil, chives, and more. A quick snip of basil adds color and great flavor to soups and vegetables, fresh, chopped chives taste superb on a baked potato, and perky parsley brings beauty to any entree.

One of the joys of having a garden is sharing its bounty to bring joy to others. Bill's parents, who live in Florida, have a huge, luscious orange tree in their backyard. Often when we visit, his mother will bring in fresh oranges from outdoors and lovingly squeeze their sweet juice for a delicious beverage. I know of another woman who always plants more beans and corn than she needs. When her crops are ready to be picked, she packs the excess into grocery bags and delivers them to the city mission.

"The cook in the home has the opportunity to be doing something very real in the area of making good human relationships."
— Edith Schaeffer

TANTALIZING KITCHENS

Though the delicious tastes of food or beverage can be savored anywhere in our homes, the kitchen is where the tantalizing begins. It is here that we drop off our grocery store finds, and stock our refrigerator, freezer, and pantry shelves with whatever pleases our taste buds. Here, we clean, chop, stir, simmer, sauté, boil, bake, broil, marinade, microwave, toast, and taste the foods we have selected. And here is where we wash our dishes, pots, and pans for another meal yet to come. The kitchen is the room in which we can demonstrate perhaps the greatest labor of love to our families, friends, and ourselves — by preparing tasty, healthy foods.

Simplify Your Set-Up

Just as it is worthwhile to first check that you have the necessary ingredients before you begin making a recipe, you must be sure your kitchen is functional and efficient before you can begin to tantalize the taste buds. Simplifying your kitchen's set-up will allow you to focus on the fun part — the food. No matter what its size, organize your kitchen in a way that is comfortable for you to cook and prepare food. Give away unneeded items and arrange your cabinet and drawer contents according to tasks you carry out near where they are stored. Use quality equipment and utensils to make kitchen tasks easy. If all you have for beating is a wobbly, old, hand mixer, you will be less excited to make that coffee cake that calls for five minutes of brisk whipping.

Live and Learn

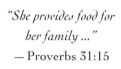

"She provides food for her family ..."
— Proverbs 31:15

Many women lack confidence in the kitchen. As with any area of life, the best way to overcome insecurity is to stretch yourself beyond today. When you stop learning, you stop living. An aunt of mine knew little more than how to boil water when she married my uncle years ago. Yet she made up her mind that she was going to learn to cook. She experimented with new recipes, learned from friends, and had others over often. She has become an excellent cook not just because she wanted to, but because she has worked at it. Plan to become a better cook each year. Ask God to help make this a fun and interesting job for you. Take a cooking course with a friend or try at least one new recipe a month. Your efforts will be well worth your while.

Whether or not you are struggling with your confidence in the kitchen, consider finding one food you enjoy cooking and let it become your trademark. My friends Sandra and Melanie make marvelous homemade bread and often share their "loaves of love" with us. Another friend has mastered the chocolate chip cookie and occasionally treats us to her tasty sweets. I enjoy making homemade candy and giving it as gifts. As you gain confidence in one area of cooking, it may give you the courage to venture into another.

One of the essential ingredients for any good cook is having delicious recipes to draw on for inspiration. Always keep a few cookbooks with healthy, easy recipes and basic cooking tips. Mark recipes with which you've had good success. Collect good and easy recipes from outstanding cooks you know. Whenever I go to my friend Sherry's home, I always leave with at least one new recipe to try. For fun inspiration, have a recipe-swapping party. I know several women who get together occasionally over a pot of soup and share tasty recipes.

Maybe you are in a season of life where your file is overflowing with recipes from twenty years ago. Consider cleaning out those you won't ever use; then plan to try those you decide to keep. Simplifying and organizing your recipe file will not only refresh your memory about some delicious forgotten dishes, but it will help you in the future to quickly locate something you want to prepare.

Once you've organized your recipes, why not share your favorite ones with young homemakers? Before Bill and I were married, I was given a recipe shower by the women in my Bible study. Each person brought five favorite recipes written on index cards and prepared one of the dishes for the ladies to enjoy at our luncheon. All the recipe cards were compiled into a cookbook and given to me to cherish over the years. It has been a rich resource!

Though recipes are helpful, don't overlook the greatest source for creativity and inspiration — God himself. The same God who created delicious food is equally available to give you fresh ideas for preparing it. One of the greatest joys in food preparation is discovering a delightful combination of tastes on your own. Let your imagination and taste buds guide you as you set yourself loose in the kitchen. You may have some failures, but chances are, you'll create some wonderful winners, too! Your taste buds are the true test for what is pleasing to you.

If you have children, let them help with cooking. Though not the fastest method, your efforts may reap great rewards. Children are more apt to experiment with what they'll eat if they have helped with food preparation. Cooking together also allows you to talk with your children while they learn, and learning to cook healthy will help them establish eating patterns that will influence them for a lifetime. As a child, I was often "in training" in the kitchen, watching or helping my mother prepare food. Much of the pleasure I gain from cooking in my own kitchen today began years ago in the home in which I was raised.

"She is like the merchant ships, bringing her food from afar."
— Proverbs 31:14

A Plan for Success

I often hear women comment that they don't mind cooking, they just dislike the planning and shopping. I have struggled in this area myself, yet I know the value of planning, so I try to make it a priority. For success in any area of life, you must first have a plan. Once the plan is in place, the shopping becomes easier. One way to simplify shopping is to keep an ongoing grocery list in your kitchen. Jot down items when they get low or when a family member makes a special food request. Then, before going to the grocery store, double check your refrigerator and pantry for needed items. This will keep your shelves well-stocked and prevent you from being caught without a needed staple.

One of the reasons many women don't cook at home today is because we fail to plan meals. After a long, hard day at home or in the office, it's hard to muster up the motivation to decide what to have for dinner. Then we fight traffic and lines in the grocery store to get the food and drag in the door and start cooking. It's no wonder we don't want to cook!

Planning menus will make your shopping experience more enjoyable because you won't have to consider the endless choices that fill the store shelves. Keep your menus simple and fresh; they will be healthier, and you will be able to better enjoy the natural flavors. Usually, the fewer items in a recipe or whole meal, the cheaper and easier it will be to prepare. A healthy meat, delicious salad, and whole grain bread or pasta make a superb, simple dinner. To save time, plan meals that can be made quickly and served more than once. When purchasing ingredients to prepare a dish like spaghetti, soup, or a casserole, buy enough to make a triple batch. Eat one batch, freeze one, and share one with a friend or neighbor. And don't forget that variety is the spice of life. If you are bored with food preparation, break out of the rut and take advantage of the boundless bounty God has created. Variety makes food more interesting to cook, serve, and eat.

If the planning and shopping are already done, a simple menu can be made in no time. I keep a list in my kitchen of menu options for which I have food on hand. In the morning, before I begin my day, I check the list and decide what to make for dinner. If the food needs to thaw, I remove it from the freezer. Once I have served an item, I cross it off my list. I have a neighbor that sometimes pops by on her way to the grocery store or farmer's market and takes a look at my posted menus for inspiration. Occasionally, I'll give her a call if I need meal motivation. Find a friend with similar taste in cooking and encourage one another with menu ideas.

A Refreshing Refrigerator

When you open your refrigerator door, does it motivate you to prepare delicious foods and beverages? The visual appeal of your refrigerator can affect your attitude toward food preparation. Does your refrigerator look like a feeding trough for you to graze in front of or a treasure chest holding delicious blessings to nourish your body? Let the inside of your refrigerator tempt your taste buds by displaying foods attractively. Food that is out of sight is often out of mind, and likely to spoil before it is remembered. Place fruits and vegetables in bowls. Use clear glass or plastic food containers to store foods. Pour beverages into glass pitchers with plastic lids. Enclose lunch meats and cheese in clear plastic bags.

Freezing is one of the best ways to preserve flavor, but even frozen foods don't last forever. Be sure to store foods in moisture-proof packaging such as plastic containers, freezer bags, or heavy foil. Mark the contents and date clearly on packages before freezing. Bread, poultry, pork, fish, and shrimp should be eaten within six months, and beef can be stored for up to twelve months. Cooked foods should be eaten within four to six weeks to assure the freshest flavor. For a touch of healthy, homemade goodness, serve a fresh salad and roll with a frozen dinner. If you serve a frozen dinner one night, try to serve a fresh-cooked meal the following evening.

"The eyes of all look to you, and you give them their food at the proper time."
— Psalm 145:15

A Fresh Start

Though canned, dried, and frozen foods supply today's tables with many options, fresh food is always the best for our bodies! When preparing foods, start with the freshest ingredients possible to assure the best natural flavor and most nutritious contents. Frequent a local farmers' market or produce stand to buy seasonal produce. Fresh fruits and vegetables in season are at their highest flavor and their lowest price. To know what is in season, look for fruits and vegetables that are plentiful, healthy-looking, and reasonably-priced. Cool months call for apples, citrus, potatoes, onions, and carrots. Warmer months welcome fresh berries, melons, corn, and tomatoes.

In many other countries, people still shop daily or several times weekly in open air markets for fresh fruits, vegetables, meats, and breads. In general, these people are healthier and more trim than many Americans living on processed foods. The closer a food is to its natural state, the better is for you. It's simple: God created our bodies, and he created the foods our bodies need to live life to the fullest.

Make the most of the life he has given you and your family and eat properly. When you do, you feel and look better, and that undoubtedly affects your home atmosphere.

Perhaps God purposely made vitamin- and carbohydrate-rich fruits and vegetables especially beautiful and colorful so we would be drawn to partake of them often. One thing is for sure, the more fresh fruits and vegetables we can pack into each day, the better off our bodies will be.

"Seeing is deceiving. It's eating that's believing."
— James Thurber

Flavorful Fruit

Fresh fruits are a perfect natural way to satisfy the sweet flavor our taste buds crave. God has created many fruits in vivid colors and varied textures for us to enjoy: pineapples, papaya, kiwi, cherries, oranges, grapefruit, mangos, melons, bananas, berries, apples, and more.

To assure fruit will have the most flavor, it's important to eat it at its peak in ripeness. Carefully hand select your fruit. I often pick a few ripe pieces of fruit and a few pieces that are not quite as ripe. The ripe ones are ready to eat, and the others will be ripe and ready to eat when we need them in several days. Check for ripeness of fruits such as peaches, plums, pears, and nectarines by placing them in your palm and gently squeezing. If fruit gives to light pressure and smells sweet and delicious, it's ready to eat. For melons like cantaloupe and honey dew, gently press on the stem end. Serve melons at room temperature for the fullest flavor. For the juiciest citrus fruit, select the heavier ones. (The heavier the fruit, the more juice it contains.) I usually place unripe fruit in front of my kitchen sink where I can enjoy its beauty while the sunshine slowly ripens it. To ripen fruit quickly, place it in a loosely closed brown paper bag at room temperature.

We hear it often, yet over one-third of Americans still don't heed their bodies' need for breakfast. As important as it is, preparing breakfast need not be a big deal. Fruit is a great, quick way to bring food and fiber to your body in the morning. For me, breakfast is usually a simple piece of fruit, like a banana, an apple, or a fruit smoothie made of blended yogurt, fruit juice, and fruit. Even if you don't feel hungry, try to begin your day with breakfast. It will jump-start your digestive system into working more efficiently throughout the day.

Some of the most delightful fruits of the spring and summer are berries. Take advantage of strawberries, raspberries, blackberries, and blueberries when warm weather comes. Luscious berries will be plump, vibrantly colored, and unblemished. Strawberries, raspberries, and blackberries are quite delicate and should be eaten soon after you buy them, while blueberries are a bit sturdier and can last longer. Try to avoid berries in containers stained by leaking juice; they are usually overripe or damaged. If strawberry leaves are brown, berries are apt to be bitter. Berries do best unrefrigerated and stored in a cool, dark place. If you do refrigerate them, don't rinse them until you're ready to eat them — rinsing and storing encourages mold. Berries are delicious plain, with a touch of cream or whipped cream or topped on a cereal. (My beloved berry is the rare raspberry.) All-fruit preserves are terrific as a tasty, healthy spread on toast, bagels, or croissants.

Fresh, sweet, firm grapes are also among my favorite fruits. Red, green, or black, I love their smooth, cool, sweet taste. Whenever I am looking for grapes, I touch them for firmness and taste them for sweetness. If they are firm and sweet, I pick up a bunch and gently shake them for freshness. Fresh grapes should cling tightly to the stem. If the grapes pass my quality-control test, I bag up a bunch to take home. Once home, I rinse the grapes thoroughly and place them in a covered glass dish in the refrigerator. Grapes are a quick, healthy way to lend color, texture, and flavor to a salad. Add fresh grapes to tuna, shrimp, chicken, or pasta salad for an unpredictable burst of sweetness. For a delicious, care-free lunch or dinner, serve grapes with a wedge of cheese and fresh French bread. Or serve a cluster of grapes with a muffin for an effortless breakfast. You can even freeze fresh seedless grapes for a cold, sweet snack.

"Do you not know that your body is a temple of the Holy Spirit . . . ?"
— 1 Corinthians 6:19

Vitamin-Rich Vegetables

Vegetables were among the first foods God created. To me, this suggests they should be a priority in our eating today. To assure maximum flavor, freshness, and vitamin content, choose vegetables with rich, bright colors that are firm to the touch. The darker and richer the vegetable, the greater the nutrients it holds. Select smaller vegetables for more tender texture and better flavor; as vegetables grow larger, they become tougher and less tasty.

The healthiest way to eat many vegetables is raw. Raw vegetables can be delicious alone or with a dip. When cooking vegetables, I prefer to steam them lightly in a small amount of water with lemon juice in the microwave or sauté them on the stove in lemon butter. If I steam them, I quickly drain and rinse in cold water and dab them with a pat of butter. Then I top them off with a sprinkle of Mrs. Dash's seasoning and they're ready to eat. Cooking lightly maintains the necessary nutrients and freshest flavor, and the lemon juice will help keep the vegetable's natural, vibrant color.

"Better a meal of vegetables where there is love than a fattened calf with hatred."
— Proverbs 15:17

Some vegetables, like carrots, potatoes, onions, and mushrooms, are available and abundant year-round. Though these vegetables are kitchen staples for any time of year, I try to take advantage of them in the fall and winter, when there are fewer fresh choices. Celebrate fall with a crock pot of vegetable soup or beef stew. I make my beef stew with beef chunks, potatoes, carrots, and onions, and allow it to simmer all day in a crock-pot in a mixture of dry onion soup mix and one cup of water.

For a great ready-to-eat, healthy snack, keep a bag of pre-peeled, miniature carrots on hand. For a vibrantly colored side dish, lightly sauté miniature carrots in butter, brown sugar, orange juice, and basil. It's simple, yet tastes sensational!

Potatoes are the most consumed vegetable in America. It's not surprising; in addition to the ever-famous American french fry, preparation possibilities for potatoes are endless. They can be served hot or cold, as a side or main dish, or in a salad. Be creative with this economical and flexible vegetable. For an easy hot dinner, load large baked potatoes with fresh, steamed vegetables like broccoli, mushrooms, onions, and carrots, and top with cheese, sour cream, or cottage cheese. For a tasty summer side dish, a big batch of potato salad is always a treat and can be enjoyed for several days. Celebrate spring with new potatoes, steamed in butter and coarse black pepper and tossed in fresh dill.

Though onions are often avoided for their aftertaste, we would certainly miss the enhancing flavor they bring to many foods. Even the Israelites wandering in the wilderness complained of missing the leeks, onions, and garlic they enjoyed while slaves in Egypt. Experiment with different onions. I use chopped leeks to give soups a mild, yet somewhat sweet taste. Scallions work well raw with dip or finely chopped and sautéed with other foods. Try fresh, frozen, or dried chives in baked potatoes or in egg or seafood dishes to bring out color and a delicate onion flavor. Purple onions beautifully enhance salads and sandwiches. When available, use sweet onions like Vidalias. I bake these sweet onion delicacies whole in butter for a tasty summer side dish.

Garlic is perhaps the most-loved member of the onion family. It gives great flavor, raw or cooked. When making a vegetable salad, rub a peeled clove of garlic inside a wooden salad bowl before adding greens. I learned this trick years ago, while watching a waiter prepare a Caesar salad tableside. For a great-tasting seafood splurge, sauté fresh scallops or peeled shrimp scampi in minced garlic and butter.

"There is no such thing as a little garlic."
— Arthur Baer

Tossed in salads or sliced on top of pizzas, in egg dishes, or in sauces, mushrooms bring a mellow, pleasing flavor to foods all year long. I often sauté sliced or whole mushrooms in burgundy cooking wine to top beef or in white cooking wine to top poultry or fish. For an outstanding appetizer or side dish, fill hollowed-out mushroom caps with chopped spinach, garlic, and grated Parmesan cheese. Broil the mushrooms until the filling is slightly crunchy. Though easy to prepare, others will think you are quite the gourmet!

Most summertime meals at our home include juicy tomatoes. Take advantage of the tasty sizes and shapes of different kinds of tomatoes when they are in season. Try to avoid using tomatoes when they are out of season or wrapped in plastic — their flavor is usually disappointing. I love the plum tomato for its small size and sweetness. It's perfect to slice for sandwiches, firm enough to eat whole like an apple, and delicious pureed to make tomato sauce. Beefsteak tomatoes are large and make a simple summer side dish when sliced and topped with chopped parsley for color. Cherry tomatoes are fun for a "baby burst" of tomato taste. Try lightly sautéing whole cherry tomatoes in olive oil, seasoning them to taste with fresh ground pepper and salt. If eaten raw, ripe tomatoes have the best flavor when served at room temperature.

The various tastes of squash can be satisfying no matter what the season. In the fall and winter, I sometimes slice an acorn squash in half, discard the seeds, and steam it in the microwave with butter, brown sugar, and cracked peppercorn. In the spring and summer, I may stir fry or steam a colorful combination of yellow crookneck and green zucchini squash. I will also chop it up raw in a fresh salad, or slice and serve it as an appetizer with dip.

The cucumber is another crisp vegetable that is great for serving raw with dip. I often marinate cucumber and purple onion slices in cider vinegar, water, and Mrs. Dash seasoning as part of a summer meal. You can also buy raw pickling cucumbers and eat one whole for a healthy, crunchy snack. They have the crispness of a pickle without all the salt.

When serving vegetables, why not add color, interest, and flavor by creating a serving dish out of an edible vegetable? Try a small cabbage head hollowed out for dips, a large beefsteak tomato filled with chicken, tuna, or shrimp salad, or a green pepper stuffed with ground beef and rice and cooked. Enjoy every bite!

Satisfying Salads

Salads are an easy way to eat more fruits and vegetables throughout the day. Salads need not be dull; they can be as vast and varied as the foods available. When it comes to a salad, anything goes! Let your taste buds take the lead. Try to buy healthy ingredients using fresh fruits and vegetables, lean meats, poultry, or seafood, and legumes, like kidney or garbanzo beans. Create a new salad or add to your old favorites. During the cold months, I prepare a salad to accompany our meal almost every night we eat at home. During the warmer months, a cold salad, like Caesar salad with sliced grilled chicken is often the main course of our dinner.

Most salads begin with greens. To build the most flavorful and interesting salads, use a tasty mixture of leafy greens. Combine tangy greens, like radicchio, with those milder in flavor, like Boston lettuce. Try crisp greens, like endive, with tender varieties, like watercress. Or mix pale greens, like Bibb lettuce, with those flashier in color, like arugula. As with all vegetables, the darker the greens, the greater the nutrients. I have found that fresh greens last longer if washed, wrapped in paper towel, and refrigerated as soon as I get them home. I am also more likely to make a spur-of-the-moment

"Food is a necessity. Preparing it is an art."
— Rosie Daley

salad if clean greens are on hand. The more convenient we make healthy eating, the more we are apt to eat healthy.

Precut and prewashed greens trim time involved in salad making. Available in the produce section of most grocery stores, they come in convenient packages of ready-to-use spinach, lettuce, and slaw mixes and cost only a few pennies more. If their convenience will encourage you to make more salads, then by all means, take advantage of prepared greens. Choose packages carefully to assure freshness. For an instant salad, cut a wedge of iceberg lettuce and drizzle on your favorite colorful dressing. This simple salad is the house salad served at one of our favorite hole-in-the-wall seafood restaurants in Florida. Though not the most interesting salad, it wins the award for being the quickest!

When creating salads, keep ingredients on hand that will add texture, color, and flavorful interest. I often toss a small cluster of toasted nuts or sunflower seeds into a salad. Slightly toasting the nuts right before adding them brings out their flavor. I may toast slivered almonds and toss them in with Boston lettuce leaves, tangerine sections, and purple onion, or throw toasted walnuts or pecans in with apple slices, crumbled blue cheese, and spinach leaves.

Olives are another quick way to add unexpected zip to a salad. Black olives are mild, while green ones are tangy. You can save time by purchasing olives as you will serve them — whole, sliced, or chopped. I usually keep several cans of black olives in my pantry to add to a salad or spaghetti sauce or to top a vegetable pizza. Green olives add a tasty zest to both green salads and pasta salads.

"In the house of the wise are stores of choice food and oil . . ."
— Proverbs 21:20

Oils, Spices, and Herbs

A dressing is the final touch to a delicious salad. The most important thing about a dressing is that it should enhance the salad flavors, not drown them. Also important is that the salad greens be dry so the dressing oil will adhere to them. Start out with a little dressing, toss well, and taste. If more dressing is needed, add a touch more. There are unlimited ready-made salad dressings available today, many of them nutritious as well as delicious. Still, it takes little effort to make your own. Experiment with flavored oils. I use a small amount of olive oil as the base for my salad dressings. Try

adding soy sauce or Dijon mustard to a mixture of coarse black pepper and olive oil. Both make delicious vinaigrettes.

I like to vary my vinegars according to the flavor I am trying to achieve and the ingredients I am seasoning. With few calories and no fat, vinegars are a great way to give vitality to many dishes. They come in many flavors and colors. For a somewhat sweet flavor, try rice or raspberry vinegar in green salads with fruit. For a tangy taste, try red wine or tarragon vinegar in salads with vegetables. For a citrus zing, replace vinegar with the fresh-squeezed juice of a lemon, lime, or orange.

There's nothing like the perky taste of pepper to add spice to almost any dish. Often, in lovely restaurants, the waiter will ask if you care for fresh ground pepper to top your salad or entree. I always accept. I love the smell and taste of pepper, as well as the texture and eye appeal its dark, coarse grounds give. If you enjoy the taste of pepper and want its full flavor, buy a good pepper mill and grind your own peppercorns. For extra-coarse, cracked pepper, crush peppercorns in a brown bag with a rolling pin. Coat steaks, roast, or fish with the cracked pepper before cooking — the flavor is marvelous. Simmer whole peppercorns in long-cooking dishes like soups and stews to slowly release the pepper flavor.

Salt also greatly satisfies the taste buds. Though God created salt, and it is indeed good, it should be used in moderation. The purpose of salt is to enhance or bring out the flavor of other foods, not overpower them. Many prepared foods today already have salt in them. I may add a pinch of salt to season a soup or sprinkle a little on a piece of melon to draw out its sweetness.

Fresh herbs are by far tastier than dried herbs, but certainly not as economical or long-lasting. Try using sprigs of fresh herbs like basil and mint in salads. They can be purchased in most produce sections. When using dried herbs for cooking, you only need one-third as much as when using fresh. Occasionally treat your taste buds to the pleasant flavor and fragrance of fresh herbs.

Delicious Dairy Foods

A glass of cold milk, a scoop of luscious ice cream, and a swirl of wonderful whipped cream are all flavorful to our taste buds. Though

"So whether you eat or drink or whatever you do, do it all for the glory of God."
— 1 Corinthians 10:31

our bodies require small amounts of these items, they are delicious. For a delightful winter appetizer, I slowly warm Brie cheese topped with sliced almonds and serve it with French bread. In the summer, I like to take light cream cheese and mix it with garlic powder and lots of fresh ground pepper to make a cold, tasty spread for celery sticks, carrots, or crackers.

Butter is very satisfying, and, when used in moderation, can turn a tasty food into something tremendous. Butter adds a burst of rich flavor to fresh bread, vegetables, meats, poultry, fish, or pastas. For a tantalizing taste, keep flavored butters on hand. Try sprinkling jalapeno, onion, black pepper, basil, and parsley onto a stick of softened butter. Mix, roll into a log, and freeze. Use a pat on broiled meats, poultry, or fish, or stir it into vegetables or pastas.

"Eat breakfast like a king, lunch like a prince and dinner like a pauper."
— Adelle Davis

TANTALIZING DINING ROOMS

The kitchen work station may well be where our meals are born, but it is at the dining table where they are most fully enjoyed. Baked bread is broken here. Filled glasses are lifted. Simmered soups are sipped. Roasted meats are eaten. With the comfort of food and the communion of family or friends, lives are blessed at the dining table.

Setting the Stage

Whether it is a sturdy pine farm table or a graceful mahogany Queen Anne table, your dining table is merely the stage platform. How the stage is *set* helps to tantalize the taste buds. A set table sends a message of love, care, and preparation. When I am invited to someone's home and see a table set for us to eat, I am touched by the time taken to prepare for our visit. Small gestures mean so much. Even if you are eating alone, value the life God has created — yours — and set a pretty place for yourself to eat. Food tastes better when there is beauty to behold. A well-set table heightens the anticipation of the meal and whets the appetite for the tastes to come.

One way to set the stage and tantalize our taste buds is to create an edible centerpiece. A basket or bowl filled with colorful, seasonal fresh fruit or vegetables is a good way to enjoy the beauty of God's bounty. I have a ceramic bowl in the center of my dining table that I fill with fresh produce for us to eat that week. Our eyes and nose, as well as our taste buds, are tantalized by their appearance, texture, and fragrance. Try using squash and small pumpkins in the fall. Green or red apples add color to the dark, cold winter. Lemons or limes light up the spring. Peaches, plums, and pears add sweetness to the summer centerpiece.

For a celebration or birthday meal, let the person being honored select the menu. Serve their favorite food on a "You are special today" plate or a favorite beverage in a "You are special today" mug. But don't save special mealtime touches just for grand celebrations. If you have china, silver, or crystal, enjoy them frequently. Life is today. Live it to the fullest! I use my grandmother's silver tableware every day to eat. As I set my table, it reminds me that today is a gift, a time to cherish and be grateful for. As Scripture tells us, today is the day that God has made, and we need to rejoice and be glad in it and make the most of it. The little touches we do to set a pleasant dining place can enhance the meal and maybe even uplift a discouraged heart.

Make it an important ritual to sit when eating meals; it will set the tone for your mind-set and your meal. One of my favorite Bible stories is Jesus' miracle of feeding the thousands with five loaves of bread and two fish. An interesting detail that often goes unnoticed is that before Jesus broke the bread and offered thanksgiving to God, he asked that the people all be seated on the grass. That was no small task, since there were five thousand men alone, with many more women and children. I would imagine their sitting turned chaos into order and better allowed the people to witness the awesome miracle about to take place. Jesus must have known that to stand and eat can never fully satisfy. It doesn't allow you to relax and enjoy the flavor and the eating experience.

In addition to sitting down when you eat, try to eat with others whenever possible. Though I occasionally treasure a time of eating by myself, it can be quite lonely if it's the normal routine. A meal shared with others is ultimately a more satisfying experience. In Diane Ackerman's book, *A Natural History of the Senses*, she appro-

"The smallest deed is better than the grandest intention."
—Larry Eisenberg

priately refers to taste as the "social sense." Eating lends itself to celebration and interaction. Much ministry can take place over a meal. An added benefit of eating with others is that you are more likely to eat healthy. If you live by yourself, start a supper club and take turns cooking. Enjoy good food with good friends.

When you sit down to eat dinner, try to always light a candle. The strike of a match takes a mere second, but does wonders for setting the stage of a meal. The quiet flicker of the flame will calm you as you eat, allowing you to digest your food more slowly as you linger over your meal. Eating should be an experience that causes you to not only stop and savor the tastes God has created, but to savor life itself. It takes twenty minutes for the brain to register satisfaction and a feeling of fullness. The slower you eat, the less you will need to feel full and satisfied. A glowing candle can be a gentle reminder to slow down.

Prepare simply.
Present beautifully.

Perhaps the greatest way to tantalize the taste buds is to serve food attractively. Think of your plate as the canvas and your food as the artwork. You are the artist and can create whatever pleases you. The plate you choose, and the color, texture, and shape of the food you serve can make a meal more appealing. In the summer, I like to serve big chunks of bright red watermelon with mint leaves on my green majolica plates. The plates look like watermelon rind as they frame the sweet fruit. I recently planned to serve shish kebabs for dinner, but was out of any colorful vegetables like green pepper and cherry tomatoes. I had only chicken, mushrooms, and onion for the skewer, with rice as a side dish. I scratched the shish kebabs before I tried to prepare them; even if they would have tasted wonderful, they would have looked unappetizing.

Visualize your meals before your prepare them. Keep color in the forefront of your mind when shopping. God has made an endless range of foods in a rainbow of colors. Enjoy his colorful blessings! Toss pretty red and yellow peppers into your stir fry beef or add purple beet slices to your green garden salad. Rather than dumping a mixture of fruits into a bowl for a salad, try arranging them onto a fruit platter. Keep color balanced. Let the eyes dance around your plate as they take in the delightful surprises of different color, shape, and texture. A white plate framing a seasoned, grilled pork chop, sliced red tomatoes, and steamed, slender, green asparagus can be simply spectacular.

Garnishes are to food what accessories are to furniture — the finishing touch. Experiment with garnishes. Try fresh fruit, flowers, vegetables, and lettuce leaves. Observe how restaurants display and accent with garnishes. I like to use Italian parsley as a garnish. Its green leaves add interest and color to a plate holding an omelet oozing with fresh vegetables or fresh fish sizzling hot off the grill. Mint sprigs work well as plate garnish, too, and both parsley and mint can be eaten after a meal to freshen the breath. For a colorful salad garnish to tender lettuce greens, add a pansy or a few rose petals. I first experienced a flower garnish at a lovely dinner reception where two pansies delicately topped each salad. Most were hesitant to try, but I dug in and discovered they are not only beautiful, but delightfully tasty! Expand your eating horizons by trying something new.

Sweet Treats

Once you've enjoyed a beautiful, flavorful meal, it's not uncommon to crave a taste of something sweet to fully satisfy your taste buds. I like to serve a small scoop of lemon, lime, raspberry, or orange sherbet for a very light, refreshing dessert. Some fine restaurants even serve a petite dish of sherbet between courses to cleanse the palette of previous flavors and refresh the mouth for the tastes to follow. Last Christmas, after a filling meal, I served a simple scoop of lime sherbet topped with a maraschino cherry and a hot sugar cookie. Everyone loved it. After a dinner of Chinese take-out, try serving a small dish of orange sherbet topped with mandarin orange sections for a perfect accompaniment to the fortune cookie.

Another light dessert is fresh seasonal fruit. Try juicy peaches and cream or succulent strawberries with tender slices of peeled green kiwi. Combine honeydew balls, blueberries, and green grapes and toss them in lime juice with fresh mint leaves for a treat that's naturally sweet.

For a fun dessert sure to tantalize the taste buds, dip fresh fruit on toothpicks in brown sugar, powdered sugar, coconut, caramel, or yogurt. As an easy dessert, I serve tart, green Granny Smith apple slices with warm caramel sauce. Or try banana chunks dipped in hot fudge and rolled in peanut pieces.

Make a delightful dessert by jazzing up crepes, waffles, pancakes, pastry puffs, angel food cake, or shortcake with ice cream or whipped cream and fresh fruit. (Save time with ready-made crepes, cakes, frozen waffles, or pastry puffs.) I once attended an evening bridal shower where the dessert was a wonderful Belgian waffle bar with all sorts of delicious toppings. Creative ideas make an occasion more memorable! I love to prepare strawberry shortcake and top it with bright red strawberries. Sometimes I'll make the shortcake with Bisquick and serve it hot. Other times, I may slice a store-bought angel food cake. You can also try the same idea using chocolate cake and raspberries.

"And after taking some food, he regained his strength."
— Acts 9:19

For an extra tasty surprise, use flavored whipped creams, like chocolate or strawberry, available in most dairy departments. I buy frozen pastry puffs and cook them while we're finishing dinner. Once they're cooked, I remove their caps and top the warm puffs with a scoop of cold vanilla ice cream and hot fudge sauce.

One of my all-time favorite winter desserts is bananas Foster. It's a simple and scrumptious dessert that warms hearts and stomachs, yet costs very little. Simply slice bananas in half lengthwise, melt butter, brown sugar, and cinnamon and pour over bananas. Coconut can be added too, if desired. The bananas can be sautéed over the stove or baked in the oven. I usually bake them very slowly while we are eating dinner and then serve them on top of vanilla ice cream. Mouths will be watering for more!

Another easy, impressive sweet treat ideal for summertime is to simply layer ice cream sandwiches in a flat pan, top them with Cool Whip and Heath Bar bits, repeat another layer of ice cream, Cool Whip and candy bits, and freeze. Before serving, remove them from the freezer to let them slightly thaw. Before serving, drizzle the tops with hot fudge sauce. The taste will be out of this world, but the work won't make you out of your mind. My kind of cooking!

If company is coming, and you need an easy dessert to feed a hungry crowd, why not try a trifle? This sweet, layered luxury can be made of whatever your heart desires. Start with a large, clear glass bowl. Alternate layers of your favorite treats like unfrosted cake cubes, fruits, pudding, whipped cream, and chocolate bar bits. Drizzle the trifle with chocolate sauce or thawed frozen strawberries in juice and refrigerate it overnight for ingredients to congeal.

TANTALIZING LIVING ROOMS

One of the easiest ways to bring variety and pleasure to the foods we eat is to vary the room setting. Because most of us love to eat and want to enjoy life and our homes to the fullest, why not occasionally eat where we most often live: our living rooms?

Many homes today are designed with the kitchen and living room open to one another. This floorplan is wonderful. It makes food preparation much more pleasurable when you can visit with others nearby or simply enjoy looking out over the rest of your home. Even if your kitchen and living room are adjacent, an occasional change in dining perspective is fun. I am especially drawn to dine in our living room when the crisp chill of fall or winter is in the air. I love the coziness of eating in front of a roaring fire. When space allows, consider including a small, round table, a game table, or a flip-top table in a corner of your living room for occasional dining. If your living quarters are limited, use your coffee table, lap trays, or portable television trays for flexible eating places.

Often on cold winter nights, I will clear our coffee table and set it for dinner. We sit on the floor and eat in front of the warm fire. If you are considering purchasing a coffee table, keep in mind that it's more comfortable to sit and eat at a coffee table that allows you to stretch out your legs beneath it. I also keep about twenty rattan lap trays on hand. When we have too many guests to seat, or if I simply want a casual atmosphere, I give them to guests so they can eat from their lap wherever they please. No doubt, if there is a fire flaming in the fireplace, that's were friends and family flock first!

Appealing Appetizers

When we have time to relax before dinner, I sometimes will prepare a small appetizer to nibble on in the living room while dinner is

"Relaxation, communication, and a measure of beauty and pleasure should be part of even the shortest of meal breaks."
— Edith Schaeffer

cooking in the oven. Bill and I can sit on the sofa and talk about the day, tantalizing our taste buds with a tasty snack while tempting aromas seep from the kitchen. A simple bowl of pretzels or popcorn, fresh vegetables and dip, or cheese and crackers are all it takes for a special treat. Appetizers can set the tone for the evening. If we have guests to our home, I serve an appetizer in the living room before the meal. The little effort of taste puts everyone at ease.

If you don't have young children at home, place a wooden bowl filled with different sizes, shapes, and flavors of nuts in your living room. Put out a nutcracker and a pick so that family and friends can help themselves. God has created so many delicious, varied nuts — pecans, walnuts, hazel nuts, and almonds, and more. Enjoy tantalizing your taste buds with nuts as you sit and enjoy life!

A Gracious Greeting

The simple act of preparing a beverage for anyone in your home is a warm and gracious gesture that always says "welcome." Whether it be a weary husband, a wound-up little one, a weeping friend, or yourself after a wild day, a warm or cool beverage at the right moment can quench the thirst and refresh the spirit.

Last year, I was working on a rather large design project. Every time I was in my client's home, no matter if I was measuring windows, moving furniture, hanging artwork, or rearranging accessories, she was there to encourage me with an invitation for a beverage. Her thoughtfulness made me feel at home. Next time a service person comes to your home to work, why not serve him or her by offering a beverage? Through your kindness, let your home be a witness for the love of Jesus Christ.

As with food, beverages are best for our health when they are as natural and as fresh as possible. The greatest liquid for us is perhaps the one we are least likely to ask for if given a choice: cool, pure, drinking water. In the world that God has created, he made far more water for us to drink than any other liquid. God designed our bodies to require water in order to function properly and to flush impurities out of our system. Though we can survive for months without food, we can live without water for only a little over a week. Retrain your taste buds to enjoy the fresh taste of drinking water. The more

"Food is the most primitive form of comfort."
— Sheilah Graham

you drink, the better you'll feel. If your tap water isn't tasty, and you don't have a water filter, buy drinking water. Keeping a cold pitcher of water in your refrigerator will remind you to drink it often.

Keep plenty of chilled, fresh fruit juices on hand to quench the thirst of those you love. Lemonade, orange, grapefruit, apple, tomato, and grape juice are all delicious. There are also many fruit juice combinations available. For a satisfying splurge, I purchase fresh-squeezed orange juice at the grocery store or farmer's market. Though more expensive than frozen, canned orange juice made from concentrate, the taste is incomparable and the fresh juice far better for us. It's closer to the original way God created it! An ad I saw recently says it best: "Close to nature is close to perfect." After a long, hard day, treat yourself or a loved one to a glass of sweet fruit juice with a sprig of mint, or tomato juice with a leafy stalk of celery. It will revitalize you and give you the energy boost you need to finish out the day with a smile.

"'. . . and my people will be filled with my bounty,' declares the LORD."
— Jeremiah 31:14

When serving beverages to those in your home, make them as lovely as possible. A delicious garnish can turn an ordinary glass of lemonade into an extraordinary experience. For a special occasion, try trimming the rim of each glass with a ring of sugar. Simply wet the glass rim with a finger and dip the glass upside down onto a plate of sugar. Place the glasses upright in the freezer to chill and harden the sugar. To serve, fill glasses with ice and beverage, sliding a whole strawberry, orange, or lemon slice on each sugared glass. The sweet rim will surely tantalize the taste buds as you sip your drink.

In the fall, I enjoy serving fresh apple cider chilled in a tall glass on ice or warmed in a clear glass mug. Fresh cider must be used within several days after it is purchased or it will spoil and begin to have a fermented, acidic taste. For a quick cider alternative, I like to keep a jug of apple juice and some Aspen Cider Mulling Spice Mix on hand. A teaspoon of cider mix with its cinnamon and clove flavor tastes delicious when stirred into a warm cup of regular apple juice.

One of my favorite beverages to serve in the winter is spicy tomato juice warmed in a mug topped with a thin lemon slice and freshly ground pepper. It is healthy, easy, and everyone loves the zippy tomato flavor. Another favorite is a steamy mug of hot chocolate in front of a fire. Top off your hot chocolate with a swirl of whipped cream and a sprinkle of cinnamon sugar or chocolate shavings. Add a cinnamon stick as a stirrer. At Christmas time, use a candy cane as a stir stick. Children will love the special treat.

If you are a coffee drinker, your taste buds know the difference between a delicious cup of hot coffee and a dreadful one. To assure the freshest flavor, store ground coffee and coffee beans in airtight containers. When making a pot of coffee, always start with cold, preferably filtered, drinking water and use the proper grind for your coffeemaker. Transfer freshly brewed coffee to an airtight thermal carafe to keep warm and avoid a bitter, burned taste.

Coffees are available in a variety of flavors, so make sure to sample until you find your favorites. For an after-dinner beverage treat, serve cups of decaffeinated coffee. Then pass around a tray of small bowls filled with brown sugar, whipped cream, and chocolate chips to enhance the coffee's flavor.

I love the ritual observed in England and much of Europe of pausing in the late afternoon for pure pleasure to partake in a sip of warm tea. I believe many Americans are living in the fast lane, while life's pleasures pass us by. We would do well to learn from our European friends to stop and savor a moment of stillness. A pretty tray with a pot of warm tea, tea cups, napkins, sugar, cream, and a small plate of cookies or fruit will make a superb tea time. Try different flavored tea bags — lemon, orange, peppermint, earl gray, or cinnamon spice. Add a spot of cream to the tea for a full, rich flavor. Whether alone or with a friend, neighbor, or family member, the living room is a perfect spot to serve a tray for tea.

Several years ago, when Bill and I were on a mission trip to Glasgow, Scotland, we grew to love the Scottish people with whom we worked. In the two weeks and fourteen teas that we were there, I visited with them more than I ever do with people I dearly love here in Atlanta! Why? Because we slowed down long enough to sit and share life over a cup of tea.

Enjoy dispensing small amounts of sugar into your beverage by using tongs for sugar cubes or a glass, lidded sugar jar with a pouring spout. Both are fun ways to enhance the pleasure of sweetening a drink. For a sweet holiday treat, I like to mix white granulated

"Tea quenches tears and thirst."
— Jeanine Larmoth

sugar with red and green colored sugar crystals. It surprises the eyes as it satisfies the sweet tooth. And if you're looking for an alternative to sugar in hot tea, try the delicious natural taste of honey.

If you have young children, why not teach them etiquette while you have fun? A few months ago, I invited several neighborhood children to our home for a tea party at the coffee table. We used demitasse cups and poured apple juice from the tea pot. I served warm slice-and-bake sugar cookies and taught them how to gently wipe their mouths with their napkins. It was such fun to see them enjoying as children, something we, as adults, should enjoy more often. Try to take time for tea.

A Little Luxury

Life should be filled with necessities and enhanced by luxuries. While healthy food is a necessity for our bodies to function properly, sweet treats like candy are a luxury that, given occasionally, do little harm and can delight the taste buds immensely. It's when we eat more luxuries than necessities that we are in danger. I like to fill a pretty crystal jar in my living room with tasty cinnamon or lemon candies that coordinate with our home's decor. Whenever guests visit, the open jar invites them to help themselves. Bill is particularly fond of butterscotch, like his father. I keep a jar by his desk filled with butterscotch candies. It's a small gesture on my part, but to Bill, it reminds him he is loved, and that means the world to him.

When we moved into our home, I announced to the neighborhood children that the Willits have a secret drawer in our living room filled with candy for them. But there are two rules that must be followed: First, they must never ask to have something from the secret drawer; they can only be offered something. This teaches them manners and self-control. The second rule is that no one can peek into the secret drawer. It is, after all, a *secret* drawer. This teaches the children to honor privacy and learn patience. Word of our little drawer has traveled rapidly throughout our neighborhood. Though most children don't dare mention the drawer, when asked if they'd like to select something from it, their eyes light up in understanding and excitement. It takes little effort for me, but to the children, it says they are loved, and they will remember that for years.

"So I ate it, and it tasted as sweet as honey in my mouth."
— Ezekiel 3:3

I know. When I was a little girl, our dear neighbors the Lemers had a special secret drawer, and I have never forgotten it.

TANTALIZING BEDROOMS

When we are ill, the bedroom is the most comfortable, restful place to eat. But why wait until you feel awful to use your bedroom for cozy dining? If you've ever stayed in a hotel and ordered room service, you know the pleasure this little luxury can bring. Dining in this room of rest can make even the simplest of food and beverage delightful. The bedroom is the perfect, peaceful setting to escape to and relish the treat of tasty treasures to your lips.

The Lap of Luxury

If space allows, consider having a small table and two chairs in your bedroom that could occasionally be used for dining. A skirted or flip-top table work wonderfully. If space is limited, or you simply like laptop dining, use a pretty bed tray and eat in bed.

When eating in bed, use whatever type of tray you prefer. I love to give a pair of wicker bed trays as a wedding gift. Along with the gift, I enclose a note encouraging the newlyweds to serve the Lord by serving and cherishing one another. If you have a silver coffee service that seldom gets used, bring out its silver tray, dust it off, and enjoy using it as a bed tray to serve a loved one or yourself anything from a midnight snack to a marvelous meal.

Kids love to eat in bed, too. If you have school-age children, start their year off with an extra measure of home-grown love by starting an annual tradition of serving them breakfast in bed on the first day of school. What about serving a teenager hanging out on her bed studying or talking on the phone? A gentle knock accompanied by a hand offering a cold beverage and a cookie may open more than the bedroom door between you and your child. For an occasional treat with young ones, and to expedite the bedtime process, tell your children that if they'll get in their pajamas and straighten up their rooms, you will bring them a dessert

snack on a bed tray before they go to sleep. It may be as simple as apple slices or a cookie and milk. The food is not what matters. How it is served and where they get to eat it is what's fun!

Sunrise Service

Growing up, most mornings my mother would bring my father a glass of juice, a cup of coffee, and a slice of toast on a small round tray. Dad would nibble on and sip his breakfast as he dressed for the day. The act may have been small, but it nourished my father's heart as well as his body, for he knew he was loved. Being in the hotel industry, Dad traveled a great deal. When he was on the road, he could have ordered any gourmet breakfast he desired, but nothing satisfied him like my mother's little breakfast tray.

"This will bring health to your body and nourishment to your bones."
— Proverbs 3:8

Sometimes when Bill and I are getting ready for the day, I slip into the kitchen and pour two glasses of fresh fruit juice and set them in a small, white, wicker basket. Then I peel two bananas, wrap them in napkins, and lay them on a tray beside the juice basket. We'll tantalize our taste buds as we talk about the day ahead. When I was sharing this little tip at a workshop several years ago, a mother who was overwhelmed with caring for her young children and her home confided that, in the midst of her busyness, she had neglected her husband's needs to feel loved and cared for. She was going to go home and spoil him. We invest into what we value. Matthew 6:21 says, "for where your treasure is, there your heart will be also." Are there relationships in your home that you need to treasure more? How about tantalizing the taste buds of those you love?

Preparing food, let alone serving it to others in bed, is, for many, too much to consider doing. If that's the case for you, do what is manageable for this season in your life. Ask God to help you with your attitude. The attitude of the heart is the most important ingredient in any food we prepare. We can either rejoice in serving or resent it — the choice is ours. Even if the recipients don't sense our attitude, God does. Proverbs 15:17 gives us some perspective on the importance of a loving attitude when preparing food: "Better a meal of vegetables where there is love than a fattened calf with hatred."

Christ's example of servant love is humbling. I'm sure he was exhausted spiritually, emotionally, and physically, the evening before he was to be crucified. Still, he lovingly washed his disciples' feet and, with his example, made a mark in history forever.

A Cup of Calmness

After an especially stressful day or when having difficulty sleeping, treat yourself or a loved one to a cup of hot tea in bed. Herbal tea is naturally decaffeinated, and the soothing flavors and scents available will quiet your mind as you wind down your day. Try chamomile for a subtle, relaxing taste.

Some years ago, wonderful friends of ours, Colin and Colleen Green, made the most of a challenging season while Colin was in graduate school by sitting in bed late at night and sipping tea as they talked about their days. It became a flavorful ritual to keep communication open and celebrate the little time they shared.

If you are like me, you seldom have the time to sit and casually browse through the cookbooks that fill your kitchen shelves. Consider placing one beside your bed. Next time you crawl into bed early, flip through your cookbook rather than a novel or magazine. Mark recipes you would like to try. Let them inspire you as you doze off. Your dreams may just be delectable!

For a real splurge in sweetness, tantalize the taste buds of your loved ones in the same manner that the finest hotels do. It's called "turn down" service. Hotel personnel fold the bedsheets down and place a tasty bite of something sweet on the pillow. Whether it be a guest visiting or a family member needing some special "TLC," a sweet treat on their pillow is sure to satisfy.

Tiny Thought

Lord,
The bounty of food
You've created to eat
Is so vast and delicious,
So tasty and sweet.

Tips for Tantalizing the Taste Buds

Simmer soups. Learn to master at least one easy soup. Try a hot favorite, like French onion soup, in the winter, or a cool, vegetable-rich gazpacho in the summer.

Go healthy with snack attacks. Have healthy snacks on hand when hunger hits. Try fresh fruits, pretzels, popcorn, nuts, or vegetables. Set out a light snack when others come home at the end of the day.

Have fun with food! Break out of the mold of boring mealtimes. Have an indoor picnic, or a make-your-own pizza, tostada, or fajita party.

Shop wisely. Be a wise steward with your food funds. Clip coupons. Skim the Sunday newspaper for special prices on grocery items. Stock up on nonperishable items when they are on sale. Eat a snack or meal before shopping to prevent overbuying.

Savor the flavor. Set an atmosphere that will enhance your enjoyment of a tasty meal by turning off any distractions. The eating environment needs to be as calming as possible. If it is stressful, it will affect your digestion process and prevent you from fully enjoying the flavor of the food.

Bring out the baskets. Use baskets as attractive containers for serving food. Use flat baskets to hold hot casserole dishes, and baskets lined with pretty napkins to serve chips and breads. Try a small basket lined with a paper doily to hold a sandwich, fresh vegetable, and a pickle for a lunch that's quick to clean up.

Master one menu. If you don't feel confident when it comes to cooking for company, come up with one great menu that you can serve whenever you have guests. Master it by making it often.

Be a happy hostess. When practicing hospitality, keep it simple and easy by preparing as much ahead of time as possible. Serve a simple casserole, salad, and bread. Food should never be more important than the people. The more relaxed you are, the more relaxed everyone will be.

Chapter Five

~

Pleasing the Ear

Better a dry crust with peace and quiet than a
house full of feasting with strife.
Proverbs 17:1

A Word on Sound

If you played a tape recording of a typical day or evening in your home, what would it sound like? Would it have the television blasting, telephone ringing, people yelling, pots banging, and dogs barking all in one accord? Or would it be calmer and more pleasant?

After the sense of sight, hearing provides the brain with the most information about our surroundings. God has wired our ears to our brains to warn us of danger, to locate things around us, to soothe and stimulate us and bring us pleasure or pain. Sound has a powerful effect on our minds, emotions, and memories. There is perhaps no more accurate reflection of our home life than the sounds that fill our walls.

"May the words of my mouth and the meditations of my heart be pleasing in your sight."
— Psalm 19:14

Sound Soothes

Whether it be calming music, the tick of a clock, the twirl of a fan, or a loving word, all are satisfying sounds that soothe. Pleasant, peaceful sounds calm us and encourage a restful spirit. Studies have shown that surgeons who listened to soothing music while in surgery performed the best; they had lower blood pressure and pulse rates, were less distracted by external things, and were better able to concentrate on their tasks. Likewise, the more soothing the sounds we fill our homes with, the more soothing the atmosphere will be. As a result, our bodies will be less stressed, our minds will be clearer, and whatever we are doing will be more enjoyable.

Sound Stimulates

In addition to soothing us, sounds can also stimulate, excite, awaken, and energize us to respond. A blaring smoke detector stirs us in the middle of the night to move to safety. A beeping alarm clock awakens us at sunrise to roll us out of bed. A yelling family member excites us to respond in anger. A buzzing dryer signals to us to remove warm laundry before it wrinkles.

Some stimulating sounds can be motivating, some lifesaving, and others simply irritating. Creating a pleasant home atmosphere involves recognizing and including positive sounds and minimizing negative ones.

Sound Stirs Memories

Turning on the radio, you hear a song that reminds you of your carefree high school days. The chime of a clock vividly takes you to your grandparents' home long ago. The phone rings, and a voice that you haven't heard in years floods your mind with memories.

Hearing a familiar sound can instantly carry us to another time and place, filling us with the emotions we experienced back then. God has wired our brains with an incredible capacity to store memories, and sound is one of the senses that most easily stores and stirs them. As we fill our homes with satisfying sounds, we are filling the minds of those we love with a wealth of memories to treasure.

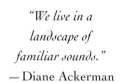

"We live in a landscape of familiar sounds."
— Diane Ackerman

Sound Today

The more advanced our technology has become, the greater the temptation to bombard our lives and homes with an overabundance of sound. We can turn on the television with the push of a button and fill a room with the sounds of a steamy soap opera, a marching band, or a newscaster halfway around the world. We can jog with our Walkman, shred our food in a processor, sweep our floors with an electric broom, and clean our teeth with a vibrating toothbrush. We can turn on jazz, rock, praise, or classical music. By choosing which sounds we will listen to, we hold the remote control to our home's atmosphere.

SOOTHING EXTERIORS

Though we live inside, many of the sounds outside can greatly affect how we feel about our homes. The humming of a neighbor's lawn mower cutting grass, the cheering roar of a little league game at a ballpark down the street, and the enticing jingle of an ice cream truck may bring back memories of your childhood home in the summertime. Perhaps the sound of a church's bell near your home comforts and assures you. Or, if you live in a big, busy city, maybe the sound of traffic and cars honking speak "home" to you.

The first home Bill and I ever lived in was a charming duplex. When we rented it, we didn't see the train tracks nearby. Initially, the rambling of trains rolling by disturbed us; but as we settled in, the sound began to add to the personality of our little home, and we welcomed it.

The Sounds of Nature

The sounds of nature can be the most soothing of all sounds. Whenever the weather permits, open your windows and let the sounds of nature fill your home. Tune into crickets chirping on a summer night, rain falling on a spring afternoon, leaves rustling in the autumn breeze, the peaceful silence of a winter snowfall. If we simply slow down and listen, we can marvel at all the sounds God created to fill our world.

For me, the sweetest sound of nature is the sound of birds outside my window. Often, while working at my desk, I open my office windows to allow the sound of singing birds to fill my ears. As I listen, I am reminded of God's love and care for all he has created, including me. The singing of a bird somehow brings encouragement with each new day.

The more inviting you make your home's surroundings to birds, the more attracted birds will be, and the more music you will hear. Lure birds by remembering that they, like us, are looking for shelter, food, and water. Birdhouses, bird feeders, and bird baths provide these basic needs for our feathered friends. Find a pretty bird feeder or birdhouse and place it near any window that you view often. I have several birdhouses and feeders near my kitchen window. Fill your feeder with sunflower seeds, one of their favorite foods. Birds also love bushes with berries and nectar-filled flowers, especially those that are red, yellow, or orange. As they discover your friendly favor, your home will become a fond place for them to perch and sing. Before long, you will be able to watch and listen as the birds enjoy their new home outside your home.

"A bird does not sing because it has an answer — it sings because it has a song."
— Chinese proverb

133

Let the gentle sound of the wind make music outside your home with the pleasant tinkle of a wind chime. Discover a wind chime beautiful to the eyes and subtle to the ears. Hang it in a breezy spot on your porch, patio, or deck, and listen to the wind whisper through it. When it comes to wind chimes, less is best. Don't go overboard with lots of different, clanging chimes that can be unsettling, not only for you, but for your neighbors as well. A simple sound is the most soothing.

"Sometimes, beauty is in the eye of the beholder; other times, it's in the ear!"
— Carole Mayhall

Welcoming Sounds

When visitors stand at your front step, how friendly are the sounds that announce their presence? The doorbell is usually the first sound guests hear when they visit your home, so don't overlook its potential for making a friendly first impression.

While renovating the exterior of our home, we needed to purchase a new doorbell. When we went shopping, we were amazed at the number of different styles, sizes, and sounds available. One store had about twenty different doorbells — everything from pleasant chimes to seasonal music to annoying buzzers. If you're in the market for a doorbell, don't assume they're all the same; choose one that suits your home and satisfies your ears.

A beautiful brass knocker can also make a wonderful statement as it taps on your front door. Select one that reflects your home's style and has a pleasant sound. For a personal touch, have it engraved with your family name to assure guests that they are at the right home.

If you have young children, rather than screaming at the top of your lungs to call them in from outdoors, why not have a friendly bell that calls them home? One of the trademark sounds of the home I grew up in was the ring of a big, black iron bell mounted on a wood post in our front yard. My mother would ring it whenever she wanted to rally family members scattered throughout the neighborhood.

This past summer, my sister and I were driving up into the mountains of North Carolina in her van loaded with kids, clothing, vacation gear — everything but the kitchen sink. We stopped at our favorite hodgepodge home store and stumbled across an iron bell similar to the one we knew as children. Somehow we made room for that bell in the van — it was too precious a memory to leave behind. When we got back home, Kelly mounted it on a sturdy wood post and tied a rope to its handle. It now adorns her home's exterior, and I always feel like running over there when I hear its ring at my home three doors down. If you like the idea of having a bell to round up the troops, but don't have a large one to post outdoors, any simple handheld bell with a hearty ring will do.

Another friendly sound that seems all but forgotten is that of a courteous chat with a neighbor. As our lives in the outside world become busier, it seems fewer and fewer of us take time to be friendly when we finally enter the private world of the home.

I recently read that one reason for the popularity of today's television talk shows is that people no longer take the time to visit with their neighbors and discuss life's issues; instead, we meet that need by plopping ourselves down in front of a screen. God has planted you where you live for a reason. Make an effort to walk outside your front door and visit with a neighbor. Talk to her about what's going on in her life. For some, this comes easier than others. If you are shy, share a plate of cookies as an excuse to chat for a minute. Be a witness in the world by demonstrating God's love and care for others. Courtesy is contagious. A friendly neighborhood starts with being a friendly neighbor.

"The lips of the righteous nourish many . . ."
— Proverbs 10:21

SOOTHING ENTRANCES

When others enter your home, what they hear not only tells them what they can expect to find but also affects how eager they will be to return. If, after a long, hard day, home is a noisy, stressful place filled with strife, chances are it will not be a place anyone looks forward to reentering. A calm, peaceful home filled with kindness and consideration, however, will be a welcome retreat.

Homecoming Sounds

Consider making it a fun family ritual that whoever drives into the garage announces his or her arrival with a quick "hello" honk of the car horn. This little sound will soon bring your heart a lift each time you hear it, knowing a loved one has made it safely back home again. As soon as you hear a honk, head for the back door to meet them with a warm and loving greeting.

Is there harmony in your home?

Another simple sound I enjoy having in my entryway is a lovely bell or string of bells tied to the entrance doorknobs with a pretty piece of ribbon. The welcoming jingle acknowledges anyone coming and going and has become a familiar greeting to our family whenever someone steps inside.

When family or friends enter your home, let background music welcome them and set the mood for the time ahead. Select music appropriate for the occasion. Play peaceful, mellow music to wind down a stressful day; upbeat music for a fun, lively time; classical music for a calming backdrop with a touch of sophistication; jazz for an easy, carefree feeling. Even if I walk in the door just minutes before Bill comes home at the end of the day, I make every effort to put on some calming music to give our home a soothing atmosphere.

If you often enter an empty home, why not welcome yourself home with a pleasant sound? Set your stereo on a timer so that it will come on before you expect to return. Or plug your stereo system into a wall outlet wired to a light switch. Put your radio on a station with music you enjoy. When you walk in and flick the switch, you will have instant atmosphere.

Nothing rings "home" to me like a chiming clock. My grandparents' home had several chiming clocks that soothingly ticked the hours away. The home I grew up in was also filled with clocks. A familiar sound to my ears was that of my father winding and pulling on the chains of the grandfather clock that stood in our front hallway. To this day, I am reminded of home when I hear that sound.

If chiming clocks don't stir up past memories for you, begin making new memories in your home with a pretty, sweet-sounding clock. Whether it be a classic clock resting on a front hallway chest, an old hanging clock adorning a foyer wall, or a stately grandfather clock greeting all who enter, find one that suits you with its sound.

A Gracious Greeting

We all need to know our presence matters. Walking in the door at the end of a weary day to another gabbing on the phone hardly makes your presence seem like a big deal. Try to make it a habit to get off the phone as soon as you hear a loved one come home. Kindly tell whomever you are speaking with that you don't like to be on the phone when your family walks in and that you can continue the conversation at another time. This simple gesture will let your family, as well as your friend, know your priorities, and both will be encouraged because of it.

When loved ones come home after a busy day, allow them to wind down before stirring up a lot of conversation. We all need time, when we get home, to shift gears, slow down, and settle our minds. Respect their need for a few private moments and they will be more likely to speak up when the time is right.

When Bill comes home, I try to meet him at the door with a warm greeting and then leave him alone as he changes his clothes and quietly looks over the day's mail at his desk. This is his time. If you are home all day with young children, you may see your husband as a rescuer for relief the moment he steps in the door. If at all possible, try to give him a few minutes before bombarding him with the day's occurrences and a screaming baby. Once he's settled, ask him to pitch in if you need help or a listening ear. Timing is everything!

Let others know you are genuinely glad to have them in your home by telling them so. Whether it be a child just home from school or a visitor sharing a meal, let them know their presence matters in your home. I'll never forget a time when Bill was teaching a Bible study in a lovely home in Social Circle, Georgia. When the hostess greeted us at the door, I told her we were pleased to be there and commented on how pretty her home was. Without hesitation, she graciously responded saying, "Well, thank you. I am so glad to have you here to share it with." Her warm words made us feel welcome and told us that people were her priority, not her possessions.

Make every effort to call those who are visiting your home by name. The simple act of remembering others' names lets them know they are loved and that their lives are important. If you are having a get-together with people who don't know one another well, set out pretty nametags and a pen on a table in your entrance. Invite each of your guests to write out a name tag and wear it. This will put everyone more at ease and encourage a friendly atmosphere.

"Everyone should be quick to listen, slow to speak and slow to become angry."
— James 1:19

Ask your regular mail and UPS deliverers and service workers their names. Write the names down, so you can remember them. The next time you see them, you will be able to address them correctly. I love to wave and say "hi" to our postman, Till. For all he does to help serve our community and our home, remembering his name is just a small gesture of kindness and appreciation. There's a good chance that when you remember another's name, they will remember your home.

Annoying Noises

"He is the happiest, be he king or peasant, who finds peace in his home."
— Goethe

I love the creaky screen door of a mountain cabin we sometimes visit. The minute I hear that creak, I know we are in for a memorable time of rest and relaxation. Quirky noises can give a home personality — to eliminate them would eliminate some of the home's character. But there can also be annoying noises in our homes that give us nothing more than a headache. Listen for and eliminate sounds in your home that irritate you. Oil squeaky drawers or doors. Fix noisy fans. Replace creaky floorboards. A simple effort can bring soothing sanity.

Try to avoid running the dishwasher, washing machine, dryer, or other noisy machinery when your family returns home at the end of the day. Appliances are notorious noisemakers and can add to stress levels. The simple gesture of silencing life's conveniences will allow your family to hear and enjoy other, more pleasant sounds when entering home. I remember a time I was talking to a friend on the phone while I had the washer and dryer going, along with who knows what else. She said, "What in the world are you doing over there? It sounds like you're working in a factory!" We may not notice noise when we're in the midst of it, but when someone steps into it from the outside world, it can be overpowering. Try to make a loved one's entrance back home as soothing as possible.

SOOTHING LIVING ROOMS

The living room is the hub of the home. The sounds that flow within these walls reveal volumes about our home lives. Whether it's laughter over a game board, roaring fans on the television, classical music on the stereo, or quiet conversation on the sofa, the sounds in our living rooms reflect our passions and priorities and greatly affect our home's atmosphere.

Serene Scenery

The furniture, fabrics, and finishes you choose for your home can affect your home's noise level. Before we moved into our current home, we did quite a bit of renovation. While we were renovating, I was also in the process of discussing the publishing possibilities for this book. Sitting on a concrete floor, talking with my publisher as my voice echoed through our empty, torn-up home, I remember thinking to myself that if they could have seen where I was speaking from they might have reconsidered wanting to publish my book! Little by little, as we laid the hardwood flooring and filled our home with soft furnishings, window treatments, and rugs, our home has become not only cozier, it has become quieter.

"If anyone has ears to hear, let him hear."
— Mark 4:23

For a soothing living room, choose furniture, fabrics, and finishes that absorb sound. Upholstered furniture and fabric draperies can enhance a room's quietness, as can paneled or upholstered walls. When it comes to flooring, carpet is the best sound absorber. When dealing with hard surface flooring, wood floors absorb more noise than floors of vinyl, tile, or stone. The harder the surface, the more it reflects noise. If you have hard surface floors, try adding area rugs to help reduce the noise.

For me, the coziest sound in any living room is that of a crackling fire. If you have a fireplace, take advantage of the charming sound it brings to your home by lighting one often throughout the cooler months. For the best burning wood, use only dry wood that's been cut and seasoned for at least nine months. We buy wood for the following fall at the end of the previous winter, to assure it is properly seasoned. For an extra snap, crackle, and pop, occasionally toss in a pine branch or cone.

Have you ever been to a lovely office and seen a beautiful aquarium adorning the waiting room? Not only are the colorful fish swimming in their exotic surroundings captivating, but the soothing hum of the motor can be quite calming. For an attractive, tranquil-sounding addition to your living room, set up an aquarium

in a prominent spot. Growing up, our family's living room book-shelves held a huge tank of interesting fish. Its motor added a soothing hum to the sounds of our home.

If you want to begin a creative collection to adorn your home, why not collect soundmakers that satisfy you? Begin a collection of pretty handbells with pleasing rings. Find old bells at flea markets or antique shops and mix them with new ones you find in gift shops or come across on family vacations. Display your beautiful, memory-filled bells in a spot looking for a charming touch of sound.

If your family is musical, collect and use musical instruments to accessorize and personalize your home. Top an old drum with a piece of glass for an interesting end table, or swag a piece of fabric through two brass horns for a whimsical window treatment. If playing the piano is your passion, enhance your living room with its beauty and soothing sound. Bill's family is extremely musical. Whenever we gather in his parents' home for the holidays, the familiar sounds of piano playing and voices singing fill their home.

Keepsake Sounds

So many wonderful moments in our lives can never be repeated. Take advantage of an audio or videotape player to record special times in your home. Tape your child's first birthday. Record his comments as he leaves and returns from his first day of school. Tape Dad reading the Christmas story in front of a crackling fire. Video your family sending their love to a relative who lives far away. The sweet, familiar sounds of a loved one's voice will keep precious memories alive.

Several years ago, Bill and I went to Kansas City to visit his dear grandmother, who was ninety-six at the time. We took along a tape recorder and taped much of our conversation with her. She spoke about her childhood, long-lost relatives, raising Bill's father, and her memories of Bill as a little boy. We learned so much that we would have never known had we not taken the time to sit and listen to her rich words of wisdom. And the best part is that we have it on tape, to pass on through the family. Honor those older generations by recording their words and wisdom. They are part of your heritage.

If you want a true earful of the sounds that fill your home, run a tape recorder unannounced during mealtime or any busy time in

"Does he who implanted the ear not hear?"
— Psalm 94:9

your home. Play it back to your family for a good laugh and maybe a little improvement. Keep it as a sound memory of this season in your life.

The Television Trap

While the sights and sounds of television can be entertaining, they can also put people in a trancelike state. Television, like food, does not have to be harmful to our well-being, as long as we are selective about what we take in. Unfortunately, in many homes the television takes center stage to family conversation and can be one of the greatest detriments to growing, healthy relationships. For a simple way to bring calmness and consideration to your home atmosphere, turn on your television to watch a few special shows, but make it the norm to then turn it off and tune into each other's lives.

Celebrate the yearly seasons with the occasional sound of a sports game being broadcasted. Swing into spring by listening to a baseball game. Kick off fall by filling your home with the sounds of football. Even if you are not an avid sports fan, show love to those who are by sitting down with them and getting into the sights and sounds of the game. They will be touched by your interest, and it may open the door for conversation. For a fuller, richer sound while viewing your television, hook the television up to your stereo speakers. You'll feel like you're sitting right in the stadium!

The Magic of Music

Bringing satisfying music into our homes is one of the simplest ways to create a pleasant atmosphere. Music is the finishing touch that completes and enhances any environment. Diane Ackerman, author of *A Natural History of the Senses*, refers to music as "the perfume of hearing." Think of how musical sound effects add to the enjoyment of a movie. How dull a story would seem without dramatic music to accompany the characters, conversation, and scenery. In the same way, playing music in our homes can make ordinary moments come alive and seem magical.

Music marks memorable occasions — birthdays, weddings, holidays, sports events, even funerals. It adds to the experience and captures the heart and emotions. When Bill and I were married, we

The kindly word that falls today may bear its fruit tomorrow.

had planned to have a wonderful picnic reception outdoors under a tent. We wanted it to be a memorable, "SenseSational" time with delicious food, fragrant flowers, beautiful surroundings, lots of hugs with family and friends, and a band playing favorite music for everyone to enjoy. With all of the details of the wedding, we went to hear the band, booked them, and left it at that. Unfortunately, neither we nor the band made any arrangements for a generator to power the sound system on the open field where our reception was. So we had no music all afternoon. Though most of the guests seemed to never miss it, I couldn't help but be disappointed knowing how much music adds to the moment.

Music also stirs memories. When I hear James Taylor's voice, I'm instantly back in my college dorm at Miami University on a spring afternoon with the window open. Keep a variety of different types of music that remind you of magical moments in your life. While in New York several years ago, Bill and I enjoyed going to the Broadway showing of "Phantom of the Opera." Now every time we play the CD, the music stirs memories of a wonderful evening in the "Big Apple."

Is there a special song that reminds you of your courtship? If so, play it for a romantic evening. In the mood to reminisce? Play music from the era in which you grew up. Many radio stations specialize in music from certain decades. Tune in to one that takes you back to "the good old days." For a fun evening, invite friends over and spin a few memories with music. We did this about a year ago, and it was an unforgettable time. We played music from our younger years and laughed at how life has changed.

"Who first created music? God the Composer. God the Musician."
— Edith Schaeffer

When it comes to music satisfaction, purchase the best sound system you can afford. Excellent sound can greatly enhance the atmosphere of your home. If possible, wire speakers into several rooms adjoining your living room and enjoy the great sound throughout your home. As technology advances, stereo systems are becoming available in smaller sizes. Stereo speakers no longer need to be an eyesore in a room; rather, they can be tucked discreetly in a bookshelf where they are certainly heard, but not seen.

Playing music that expresses and reflects our emotions is greatly satisfying. God has placed in all of us an appreciation for some kind of music. Scripture refers often to enjoying the gift of sound. Even if we are not musically talented, we can appreciate and enjoy music and the blessing it brings to life.

The Bible also mentions a *variety* of musical instruments: trumpets, cymbals, pipes, flutes, harps, tambourines, and more. Edith Schaeffer's attitude towards music in the home reflects mine: "Christian homes should not be places where nothing but a bit of sentimental music is heard, but places where there is the greatest variety of music." Fill your home with a wide range of appealing music.

As satisfying as pleasant music can be, having irritating music or other noise can be equally disturbing. Yet, whenever two or more people live together under one roof, there will be times when there are different sound preferences. For the most pleasant atmosphere, it is best to have only one thing playing at a time: CD player, tape player, radio, or television. If that is not possible, be considerate and compromise. Use a headset. Close doors. Turn the volume down. Take turns selecting music. Love one another by respecting everyone's enjoyment of certain sounds.

The Sound of Silence

"Praise him with the sounding of the trumpet, praise him with the harp and the lyre."
—Psalm 150:3

In our age of technology — where we can have whatever sound we desire at the push of a button — there is one sound that is seldom considered as an option: silence. When your mind is begging to be cleared of clutter, turn off the stereo and television and relish the sound of silence. Although God created wonderful sounds to fill the earth, he is not opposed to silence. Look at the moon and stars and clouds. They rest silently in the sky, their quiet presence peaceful and satisfying. Many people insist on having some noise on at all times. I find this sad. It is in my quietest moments that I find my greatest inspiration. My mouth is closed. My mind is quiet. And my ears and my heart are open.

Treasure silent moments in your home and encourage your family to do the same. Of course, I am not referring to the rude behavior of the "silent treatment." I mean deliberate times when electronic sounds are off and the turning of a page or a loved one's voice are all that is heard. I love to curl up on the sofa and read a good book with nothing more than a crackling fire to fill the air.

An essential ingredient in creating a "SenseSational" home is to set aside a time alone to be still before God. Make it a priority to spend time alone with God in the early morning or some other time when your home is calm. In her book *Greater Health God's Way*, Stormie Omartian says, "The more time you spend with God in quiet solitude, the better you will hear his voice guiding you and directing you in times of busyness and noise." Even Jesus slipped away from the noisy crowds to be quiet and alone before his Father. Quiet time alone with God is a key ingredient in making your home a soothing place.

"Busyness destroys intimacy."
— Andy Stanley

Taming the Tongue

Scripture has much to say about the little muscle in the mouth called the tongue. Indeed, sounds made by the tongue can build or destroy our homes. God has created women to be emotional beings and has given us a great need to express ourselves verbally — twice as verbal as men. When you put together emotions and a lot of talking, there is the potential for our homes to sound far from "Sense-Sational." The bad news is, controlled by ourselves our tongues can be dangerous and destructive. There are many homes filled with angry women and sharp words.

The good news is that, when we allow God to take control of our hearts and minds, we can use our tongues to be compassionate and constructive in the lives of those we love. It is amazing what God can do when we give him the freedom to take control of areas in which we struggle. We must also monitor all that we pour into our hearts and minds — the television shows we view, the books we read, and the sounds we listen to — realizing that sooner or later everything that goes into our minds will flow out of our mouths.

If you want family members to keep coming home with eager hearts, you need to nurture them, not nag them. Nurturing words are kind and pleasant; they stimulate growth in others. Nurturing has the best interest of others in mind — it encourages. Nagging, on the other hand, is selfish — it annoys and irritates. People nag in order to get their own way. Proverbs 21 clearly illustrates the devastating effects of a nagging or quarrelsome woman. In verse 9, it says that it is better to live on a corner of the roof than to live with a quarrelsome woman. By verse 19, it's better to live in a desert than live with her. Nagging drives others farther and farther away, if not physically, at least emotionally.

When I feel the urge to nag Bill, I have to remind myself of the saying, "Get off his back and on his team." Are you nourishing those around you with your words? If you struggle with nagging, try making a request once, then dropping it. A few words of encouragement will keep things in perspective and accomplish more than nagging ever will.

"He who holds his tongue is wise."
— Proverbs 10:19

We've all heard the adage, "It's not what you say, but how you say it." Studies show that people communicate only 7 percent with words, but 38 percent with tone of voice (and 55 percent with non-verbal communication). The tone of my voice gives my heart away. If I am discouraged, my voice drops an octave and becomes quieter and more monotone. If I am excited, it gets higher with more volume, speed, and energy. Keep a close check on the tone and volume in which you communicate in your home. Choose to not raise your voice, no matter how great your frustration. Remember, "A gentle answer turns away wrath, but a harsh word stirs up anger" (Proverbs 15:1).

Even in the greatest conditions, we all blow it now and then, especially with the ones we love the most. Try to keep a clean slate in your home by apologizing sincerely as soon as possible after an offensive incident. Humble words like, "I'm sorry, will you forgive me?" can heal a broken heart and prevent destructive walls of bitterness and resentment from building. Be an example to those you live with by humbling yourself. The more you do it, the easier it becomes. God honors a humble heart.

Another way to express love to those with whom we live is by simply listening to them. God has given us two ears and one mouth. Research shows that the average person listens to someone else speak for seventeen seconds before interrupting. Listen carefully, and respect others while they are speaking. When you sense someone in your home wants to speak about something important, give that person your undivided attention. Turn off the water. Put down the pen or dishtowel. If a child is talking, get down on their level and listen with both ears. A friend of mine's husband recently opened up to her about a painful family struggle. She offered no advice, no suggestions, only a loving, listening ear. Her husband was touched by her willingness to simply listen, and told her so. Fewer counselors would be needed if we gave the gift of listening in our homes more often.

Healthy Humor

Is laughter a familiar sound in your home? Like a ray of sunshine, laughter can lighten life's load by brightening your outlook and broadening your perspective. If the relationships in your home seem strained or uptight, perhaps you need to lighten up and enjoy a good laugh, especially at yourself. Though life can be hard at times, there's no need to take everything so seriously. Scripture affirms there is a time to weep and a time to laugh. Both are important. Rent a funny movie, relax, and enjoy life and those you love. Filling the walls of your home with laughter is a loving sound your family won't forget.

Healthy humor actually helps us by reducing stress. In contrast, unhealthy humor, like sarcasm, hurts. Sarcasm is humor at the expense of others; it may start out funny, but it ends up destructive. Sarcasm conveys disrespect and is often hurled by those who are hurting themselves. Humor can be contagious — no matter what kind it is. It always saddens me to be in a home where sarcastic remarks fly constantly. Do a sound check on the sarcasm in your home. Start by listening to yourself.

Take time to laugh — it is music to the soul.

SOOTHING KITCHENS

Most of us use our kitchens for far more than food preparation and eating. Our kitchens are a natural gathering place for homework, paperwork, or just sitting and visiting. It is in this room that family and friends often feel most at home. It is here that they come together for casual chats or heart-to-heart conversations. Keeping our kitchens as soothing as possible makes them conducive to conversation. We never know when, while we're stirring a hot pot of soup, someone may be warming up to share their heart.

Your Line to the World

The telephone was invented to enhance communication. Have a cordless phone or a phone with a long cord in your kitchen. Either will give you flexibility to work while talking. I don't usually enjoy talking on the phone, especially after a long day. I try to save time by making all my calls at one time of the day, or doing easy, quiet tasks like ironing or drying dishes while I'm talking. Try not to waste your day away on the phone. It can be an unproductive time grabber.

"Let your conversation be always full of grace, seasoned with salt . . ."
— Colossians 4:6

If you're in the market for a new telephone, buy a quality one. Not long ago, I was talking to a friend who was speaking on a telephone that made her difficult to understand — her voice echoed like she was talking through a tin can. Then she changed to another phone, and I could hear her loud and clear and enjoy our conversation. When buying a phone, select one with clear reception, the features you want, as well as a pleasant-sounding ring. Ask to hear the phone's ring before you buy it. If that's not possible, return the phone if you try it at home and are not satisfied with its sound. Set the ring volume on the lowest level that you can adequately hear. A sudden, shrieking phone can jangle the nerves.

Answer your phone with warmth and enthusiasm. This is your line to the outside world. If you want to minister to others from your home, you must be kind and considerate on the telephone, no matter how you feel or who's on the other line. If a telephone salesperson calls, rather than being rude, simply tell them you make no purchases or contributions over the phone, thank them for their call, and wish them well. If you can't answer the phone pleasantly, just don't answer it.

If you desire one, an answering machine can take messages while you're away from home or when you simply do not want to be disturbed. Choose one that has features you desire. Place your machine in a convenient spot where it won't disrupt conversation with family or friends. We have an understanding in our home that when we have visitors, we seldom answer the phone. For a while, whenever our answering machine would pick up a call, our guests could hear the caller leaving a message. Eventually, we wised up and turned down the volume control.

Quiet Your Conveniences

Along with the conveniences of today's kitchens come some disturbing noises — the dinging of the microwave, the popping of the toaster, the buzzing of the stove timer. Though there are some sounds we can't avoid, some can be minimized with little effort.

The noise level of countertop appliances varies. Usually, the better the quality, the quieter the model will be. The sounds of blenders churning, mixers beating, and food processors chopping can add unnerving noises to our kitchens. Reduce noise by placing a dishtowel around the motorized area while operating.

Have you ever been in another room while someone is emptying the dishwasher in the kitchen? It can sound like a bull in a china shop — clinking glasses, banging pots and pans, crashing silverware. Wood or laminate cabinets tend to reflect and amplify kitchen sounds. Soften the sound of dishware by placing rubber or cork tile on the shelves of your kitchen cabinets. To make closing the cabinets quieter, use soft rubber or cork bumpers on the inside edges of doors and drawers. Remember that the noise you make is amplified in others' ears, and try to put dishes away gently.

When shopping for appliances, look for models with sound control. Many dishwasher models offer quieter operation. Some food waste disposals are wrapped with insulation for less noise vibration. Ask to hear an appliance running before purchasing it.

Turning on an exhaust fan over the stove can sound like an airplane getting ready for take off. I always try to run my exhaust fan on the lowest level possible to reduce the noise but still draw fumes. If you're looking to buy an exhaust fan, be aware that most fans have a numeric rating. The lower the rating, the quieter the sound.

Even with quieter models, try to run appliances at times when they are least disturbing. Turning on the disposal while someone is talking on the phone, or running the dishwasher when you sit down to dinner can be disruptive.

Listen While You Work

If you have cooking or cleaning to do in your kitchen (or anywhere else around the house), try to make your time working as

" . . . a time to be silent and a time to speak."
— Ecclesiastes 3:7

"Take time to be quiet — it is the moment to seek God."

pleasurable and productive as possible. Listening with your ears while working with your hands can make the time go faster and the task a bit more rewarding. I like to listen to Christian radio broadcasts or teaching tapes while I'm cooking, ironing, or working in one room. They always minister to me as they stretch my mind and challenge me spiritually. If you can't seem to find time to read, but want to enjoy a best-selling book, many are available on audiotape. Purchase one at a bookstore or check one out at a local library. Take advantage of your time and enjoy listening while you work.

"Conversation skills learned around the family table carry over to the classroom, and into adult life."
— Mary Beth Lagerborg

SOOTHING DINING ROOMS

When we sit down to eat, our minds need to be nourished just as much as our stomachs do. Sounds we hear while eating may not only affect our dining atmosphere, but our attitudes in life as well. Controlling the sounds that fill a mealtime can make it a more peaceful and satisfying experience.

Make the Most of It

When you call others in your home to the dinner table, do you scream "Dinner!" at the top of your lungs and pray that everyone will come before the meal gets cold? Consider making your dinner call more soothing for all by having a small dinner bell to ring when dinner is almost ready. By the time loved ones wrap up what they're doing, dinner will be done, but no one's nerves will be. I keep a small pewter bell by my kitchen sink and often ring it to announce to family or friends that a meal is ready. The soothing ring is always a welcome sound to hungry appetites.

The sounds of a family gathered around a dining table are heard less and less frequently in many homes today. If the American family is endangered, as many statistics indicate, I believe one of the resounding reasons is the demise of the family dinnertime. I'm not referring to eating, but to the conversation and bonding that can take place over a meal. Great security comes from a regular ritual shared and enjoyed with those you love.

Much of Jesus' ministry took place talking over meals. Jesus visited in the homes of Zacchaeus and Martha and Mary, sharing important truths over meals. He used the Last Supper as a sacred time to give some of his most important instruction. Jesus realized the value of eating in an atmosphere of communication.

If eating together is not a priority for your family, you are missing out on one of the most influential sounds in your home. There's no better way to get to know one another than to dine together. The eating experience encourages intimacy. When we open our mouths to eat, our hearts and our minds often open as well.

In an interview with *Today's Christian Woman*, Marilyn Quayle attributes the good communication she and her husband have with their teenage children to the ritual established long ago of a family dinnertime. She says, "If I could pinpoint one thing that could help families, it's taking time to sit down together at dinner. Start when they're little — when they don't have a lot to say, but you have a lot to offer them — and show them you care about them and make conversation."

Make every effort to sit down with others and eat together on a regular basis. If necessary, give young children a nap and a snack to tide them over until everyone is home to eat dinner. Your extra effort will bear fruit long after the dishes are cleared. In an edition of *Focus On the Family* magazine, James Dobson affirmed the security a regular family mealtime can bring when he said, "All of us desperately need to feel that we're not just part of a busy cluster of people living together in a house, but we're a living, breathing family that's conscious of our uniqueness, our character and our heritage." Nothing can provide that foundation like the dinnertime together.

Creating a soothing eating experience requires more than just sitting down and eating together. It requires setting the right atmosphere. Avoid answering the telephone during meals, but especially dinners. Turn off the television or talk radio and turn on pleasant music. Music with slow tempo, such as classical music, encourages people to eat more leisurely and savor the tastes.

Try to keep the dining atmosphere positive. Save heavy subjects for another time. Make an effort to include everyone in the conversation. If you have young children at the table, save grown-up

"Mealtime for me is a sacred time. We share more than food around this table. We share life and being."
— Karen Mains

conversation for later. Ask open-ended questions that will encourage others to talk.

Some of your most treasured family times can occur after a meal is finished, when plates are empty and stomachs are full and you linger and laugh with those you love. Don't overlook the soothing sense of security a mealtime conversation can bring to your home.

"To speak kindly does not hurt the tongue."

Attitude of Gratitude

Learning to have a grateful spirit begins in the home. Make it a regular ritual to begin every meal with a brief prayer of thanks to God for his provision of food. Take turns saying the prayer, and encourage children to participate. However few or simple the words, a prayerful pause will allow you to reflect on God's goodness with a grateful heart.

An attitude of gratefulness should carry over into family relationships as well. How kindly you speak to others certainly affects your home's atmosphere. Use the word "please" as part of your everyday vocabulary. Make a special effort to thank family members often. Thank them for helping prepare dinner. Thank them for doing the dishes. Thank them for emptying the trash or paying the bills. A sincere word of thanks encourages those you love to keep going and let them know their little efforts are appreciated. Teach others in your home an attitude of gratefulness by your example.

SOOTHING BEDROOMS

The first and last sounds we hear each day are in our bedrooms. We may wake to music, an alarm, or birds chirping outside our window. We may wind down the day with tender words of "I love you" or "Sleep tight" or a heartfelt prayer lifted to our Heavenly Father. We may drift off to sleep in the quiet of the night or listening to God's lullaby of raindrops falling or crickets chirping. Making our bedrooms a peaceful place of soothing sounds promotes the satisfying sleep we need.

Sweet Sleep

Assuring a good night's sleep involves several ingredients. In addition to eating properly, getting adequate exercise, and having a comfortable bed, you need time to unwind mentally and quiet your busy brain. That means reducing the input of stressful sounds. After you have retired to your bedroom for the night, avoid taking phone calls. Talking on the telephone forces you to reenter the world and prevents you from mentally unwinding and getting to bed on time.

My idea of courteous calling time is from nine in the morning to nine at night. Indeed, most of us are up and awake before and after these times, but the early morning or late evening should be considered private time that need not be interrupted by the outside world. If someone calls in the middle of the night, consider it an emergency. If someone calls late in the evening, consider it impolite and don't answer. Guard your time of rest. Being in the ministry, our phone, like yours perhaps, rings often, even at night. To protect our family time, we have had to set some guidelines. We have learned that even seemingly urgent phone calls can often wait to be dealt with until the light of a new day.

To me, the most soothing bedrooms do not have televisions. The television tempts us to bring the stresses of the world into our sanctuaries and can destroy conversation or a sense of calm. Of course, when one is sick at home in bed for several days, the television may be a friendly diversion. If you insist on having a television in your bedroom, monitor your viewing. Do you automatically turn on the television when you crawl into bed? Do you fall asleep to the sound of the television blasting every night? Or do you occasionally turn it on for a special show? For a while, Bill and I got into a poor habit of watching a particular late-night television show; it was unproductive and took away from quiet moments of reading and conversation.

Although most of us would prefer falling asleep in a quiet room, it is not always possible. Whether it be distractions from another sleeper, another room, or just a restless mind, sometimes we need to tune out some kind of noise before we can drift off to dreamland. One option is to wear a pair of comfortable earplugs. Another option is to mask the noise with a constant humming sound, such as an air

"Silence is more musical than any song."
— Christina Rossetti

conditioner, small fan, or space heater. A friend of mine started turning on a small fan to lull her toddler to sleep for his nap, so that he wouldn't hear her newborn cry. Now the little boy requests the fan be turned on whenever he heads for his bed. The familiar sound soothes him.

Sleep machines that continuously play recordings of pleasant sounds of nature can help you drift off into deep sleep. Bill's sister Suzi, and brother, Rick, are both so accustomed to listening to their sleep machines that they tote them along whenever we get together for a holiday weekend. No matter your age, soothing, familiar sounds can make you feel satisfied and secure enough to fall asleep.

" . . . when men rise up at the sound of birds."
— Ecclesiastes 12:4

If you are an habitual snorer, or sleep with someone who is, chances are you're not getting a restful night's sleep. Friends of ours recently went on a wonderful vacation to a lovely hotel. Everything was perfect, except the annoying sounds of the snorer in the hotel room next door. They couldn't sleep all night! Fortunately, the snoring guest checked out the following day. To help eliminate a snoring problem, get a contoured snore pillow for the "culprit" to sleep on. The contoured foam cradles the neck and head to allow for proper breathing and peaceful sleeping.

In any home with more than one occupant, it is likely that everyone is not on the same sleeping schedule, so be sensitive and considerate to those who are sleeping. Some people are lighter sleepers than others. Tiptoe quietly. Whisper to others. Turn off the ringer of a telephone close by. Bill and I try to be considerate if one of us must wake up in the morning before the other. The one of us who has an especially early morning will lay out our clothes in the bathroom the night before to avoid fumbling through drawers and disturbing the other's sleep. It's a simple gesture of silence that conveys love and respect.

What is the most pleasing sound to wake you in the morning? It may be the words of a loved one saying "Good morning," the gurgle of a baby, or the beep of an alarm. The way you wake up can set the tone for your whole day. A survey of the wake-up techniques of Americans confirms that we all have sound preferences. Twenty-eight percent of us set our alarms on the buzzer, twenty-six percent set them to soothing music, sixteen percent of us hit the snooze button, five percent require several alarm clocks around the room, and thirty percent wake up on our own. Be mindful of how you like to wake up and make every effort to arise in the most pleasing way possible. If you like to wake to the soothing sound of music, as I do, check the station and volume when you set the alarm at night. Being a light sleeper, waking to a blaring radio can rattle my nerves before I've even rolled out of bed. Many alarm clocks have CD or tape players that can be set to wake you to whatever you choose. Why not put on a praise CD and wake up with a grateful heart?

The Sounds of Sickness

Many illnesses bring the sounds of coughs, sneezes, sniffles, blows, moans, and groans. Be prepared by keeping plenty of cough, allergy, cold, and pain medicine on hand. If congestion is the problem, a vaporizer can soothe your ears and mind as it clears your head and chest.

If you are sick and sleep with a mate, considerately offer to sleep in another room. Not only will this help keep your spouse healthy, but it will allow them to get a quiet night's sleep without your special sound effects. The healthier a home is, the more soothing it will be.

One of my fond memories as a little girl was when I was sick at home and had the privilege of keeping our family's "get-well bell" beside my bed. Even though under the weather, tingling the little bell made me feel special and loved. Its simple ring would summon my sweet mother to console me or bring me what I needed. Why not begin a family tradition in your home by spoiling a sick loved one with a designated "get-well bell"? Its soothing sound and a little "TLC" is sure to help cure any mild illness, whatever age the patient.

Talk Time

Some of the most tender times of talking can be spoken as we wind down the day. In the privacy and comfort of our bedrooms, we feel the freedom to share our deepest thoughts, feelings, and dreams. Cherish the young years of your children or grandchildren by treasuring the times you tuck them in bed. Don't rush the ritual; instead, listen, laugh, and shower them with love. Read them their favorite stories or talk to them about life. Usually, in the coziness of

"[Love] . . . is not rude, it is not self-seeking, it is not easily angered, it keeps no record of wrongs."
— 1 Corinthians 13:5

their beds, they will open up their hearts to you. Every now and then, tape record one of your "tuck in talks" and save it to listen to when your kids are too big to tuck in any more.

In addition to reading to children in bed, make reading aloud to one another a common sound. The sound of a loved one reading aloud to another speaks "unity" — knitted hearts, shared passions. Sometimes when we crawl into bed at night, Bill will read a passage of Scripture that speaks to where our lives are. A friend of mine reads to her husband at night while she rubs his back.

"Listen twice as much as you speak."
— Tim Kimmel

Inevitably, there will be times at night when you are tired and your discussions will turn to disagreement. Ephesians 4:26 urges us to not let the sun go down while we are angry. It is best to settle matters before going to bed, but there are some weary nights when continuing the conversation only leads to further frustration. When this happens in our home, Bill and I have established an understanding that we set another time and place to resume what we call our "peace talks." If possible, we plan to go out for an early breakfast or dinner date the next day to continue our discussion. Once we are rested and refreshed, we often gain a better perspective and resolve the issue faster with far fewer painful words. However you choose to resolve misunderstandings in your home, do deal with them. Don't sweep them under the rug. A soothing home is a peaceful home.

SOOTHING BATHROOMS

The sounds that flow from our bathroom walls should soothe like an oasis. Whether it's the steady sound of rushing water or a peaceful praise melody, pleasant sounds can gently ease us into the dawn of a new day and quietly calm us as we end each evening.

Water Works

One of the most soothing sounds God has made is the sound of water — trickling down a stream, rushing from a waterfall, crashing on a shore, dropping on a rooftop. Your bathroom can bring the same soothing sound every time you turn on a faucet. After a long, difficult day, turn on the bath water and listen to its peaceful sound as it rushes out of the faucet. Let the water wash away your cares as it fills the tub.

When standing under a sprinkling shower, go ahead and sing in the rain. Belt out a musical melody. Whatever others think doesn't matter. We all think we sound pretty good in the shower. Give your day a lift, and lift your voice.

As pleasant as the sound of water can be, a noisy toilet flushing can be a distraction. Some toilets flush quieter than others. If you are purchasing or replacing a toilet, keep sound in mind as you make your selection. For a quieter-sounding flush on an existing toilet, put a pretty, padded cover on your toilet seat lid. The fabric will absorb and soften the sound of flushing water. When decorating a client's bathroom, I often suggest having a matching toilet seat cover made to coordinate with the room's design scheme. Not only does it quiet the flush, but beautifies a fairly unattractive necessity.

"The mouth of the righteous is a fountain of life."
— Proverbs 10:11

Pleasant Sounds

If you have a bathroom or powder room adjacent to your living room area, assure your guests sound privacy with a vented fan. For bathrooms frequently used by friends or several family members, mount a small brass door knocker on the outside of the bathroom door. It can be a pretty accessory and gentle reminder to respect one another's privacy and knock before entering. Our powder room door holds a little brass knocker that once adorned my grandmother's powder room. I remember, as a small child, standing on a stool so I could reach the knocker on the bathroom door. I loved its tiny, tapping sound. Don't underestimate the small, soothing sounds you add to your home. Even little sounds can hold large memories.

Bring your favorite sounds into your bathroom with a portable tape or CD player. Select music appropriate to the mood you wish to attain. Listen to romantic, peaceful, easy music as you soak in the tub before turning in for the day. Play upbeat music while getting ready to go out on the town. I love to listen to praise music in my home anytime, but especially in my bathroom as I prepare for the day. Whether all instrumental or with lyrics, praise music focuses my mind and heart on the Lord. I often pop in a praise tape and meditate on it as I step into the shower.

I remember a time years ago when I was extremely discouraged and called a godly friend. She didn't try to solve my problem. She gave me the best advice a friend could offer. She suggested I sit and listen to a praise tape. I was hurting too much to pray, but I could sit and listen and let God minister to me with music. Focusing on the Lord and giving praise to him can put life in perspective, melt a hardened heart, and soften rough times. Play praise music as you begin your day in the bathroom or anytime your spirit needs a lift.

"It is good to praise the LORD and make music to your name ... to the music of the ten-stringed lyre and the melody of the harp."
— Psalm 92:1–3

Have a few, fun, familiar tunes to play during children's bath-time. The musical melody will add to the experience. One of the easiest ways to learn Scripture is by listening to Scripture memory melodies as you prepare for or wind down your day in your bathroom. Many tapes can help you store up the treasure of God's Word in your heart and mind as you sing their catchy tunes. I play a fun children's tape for bath time with my niece and nephew. One of the songs sings about the fruit of the spirit. By the age of three, my little nephew could name the fruit of the spirit and loved to sing about them at the top of his lungs.

We can also learn Scripture by seeing it and saying it frequently. Hang a verse that you'd like to memorize on your bathroom mirror and quote it out loud several times while getting ready for the day. There will come a time when you can draw on those words stored up in your heart and mind, and they will bring you comfort and strength.

Tiny Thought

Lord,
May the words that I say
And the sounds that I play
Bring harmony to my home,
and glory to you alone.

Tips for Pleasing the Ear

Make music. If you or those you love play an instrument, determine appropriate times and places for practicing. Whether it's the piano, guitar, flute, or other instrument, making music can make your home beautiful.

Whistle away. Buy a pretty teapot that whistles. When you need hot water, fill it up and listen — it will sing to you when your water is boiling.

Express your love. We can never hear enough of the words "I love you." Don't miss an opportunity to let your family know you love them.

Jingle your pillows. Stitch a bowed bell on each corner of a square pillow. Every time it's tossed, it will jingle. Make holiday jingle pillows and give them as Christmas gifts.

Sound off for safety. For maximum fire prevention safety in your home, install a smoke detector in every room that has a door that can be closed. Change the batteries annually.

Wind up a memory. For a touch of beauty and music, place a pretty music box in a little spot that invites others to wind it up.

House a feathered friend. Enjoy the sweet chirp of a canary or the smart talk of a parakeet in your home. Keep your bird in a decorative bird-cage and let its song and chatter become a part of your home's familiar sounds.

Pray aloud. Make it a nightly ritual to kneel at your young child's bedside for prayers, and also pray out loud beside or in your own bed before you go to sleep. Even a short prayer of thanks for the day lets God know you haven't forgotten his hand in your life.

Minimize vibrations. To prevent your heavy appliances like the washer, dryer, or refrigerator from transferring additional noise vibrations to the supporting floor, place rubber pads under each leg or corner of the appliance. Be sure to allow at least two inches between the wall and your appliance, and between your washer and dryer, to eliminate banging noises.

Chapter Six

~

A Touch of Comfort

*The wise woman builds her house, but with her own
hands the foolish one tears hers down.*
Proverbs 14:1

A TOUCH ON TOUCH

The instant you entered this world, touch was the first sense you experienced. Loving, tender hands reached for your head to help bring you beyond the safety and seclusion of your mother's womb. You probably let out a wail as you gasped for your first breath of fresh air. You may have heard strange and muffled noises from the doctor and your elated parents, and your eyes were more than likely filled with fluid and could not yet focus. But as soon as you lay in your mother's arms, nestled next to her warm breast and beating heart, you discovered one of our greatest and most urgent needs — the need for touch.

From the moment of birth on, touch has been a vital part of life. After all, we touch every day. We touch people. We touch things. But I would venture to say that few of us realize how important touch truly is, especially in our homes.

God felt that touch was so important that he covered our entire bodies with sensors and feelers. He intricately wired each of us with approximately five million receptors that send information to our brains about temperature, pleasure, pain, and pressure.

Unlike any other of our senses, touch can be stimulated by every inch of the body. It affects nearly all that we do in our homes. Touch can be a tender kiss, a bear hug, a gentle stroke, or a loving pat from a significant person in our lives. It can also be simply sinking into a comfortable chair, soaking in a hot bath, or curling up under a cozy quilt. When we experience a comforting touch, good things happen to us physically and emotionally.

Touch Relaxes

If you've ever experienced the luxury of a satisfying sofa, a gentle back rub, or a deep massage, you know how a touch can relax our tired, aching bodies, sometimes to the point of falling asleep! How does it work? When we encounter positive touch, whether it be touching a person or thing, the brain stops releasing stress chemicals and activates a relaxation response. As our bodies relax, our blood pressure lowers, slowing and soothing our whole system. If we want our homes to be refuges for rest and relaxation, it is important to take time for tender moments of comforting touch.

Touch Conveys Security

Little children cling to favorite blankets or tattered teddy bears. An infant who skins a knee immediately runs to a parent's loving arms. Touching something or someone familiar gives us a sense of reassurance and security, no matter what our age. A warm hug from a loved one at the end of a long, hard day communicates, "You're home now, and everything is going to be okay. It's safe here." Crawling under the sheets of your very own bed is like crawling into a comforting cocoon; you feel safe and protected from the storms of life. The ironic thing is that the more secure we feel in our home life, the more social we can be. The emotional security we receive from being surrounded by warm, loving touch gives us the courage and confidence to explore life beyond the walls of home.

Touch Satisfies

It may be a hug, kiss, hold, snuggle, stroke, cuddle, caress, massage, tickle, or tumble—they all satisfy both the giver and the receiver. When we are touched physically in a positive way by a significant person in our lives, we can't help but smile. Why? Because it satisfies one of our deepest human needs: to feel loved, needed, and accepted. Perhaps God created our bodies to require physical touch for health and happiness so that we would recognize we need others in our lives.

Though not as critical as our human need for physical touch from another person, touching comfortable *things* can also be a great source of satisfaction in our homes. This kind of touch also communicates warmth, love, and acceptance. Think about the softness of your favorite bed pillow beneath your head, of a plush sofa cushion to your back, of a cotton quilt draped over your arms and legs. Each can bring enormous enjoyment as we touch them.

The satisfaction touch brings is often a very subjective thing. Creating a comforting home includes noticing and weeding out those textures that are unpleasant to your sense of touch. Ever since I was small, two textures have been uncomfortable to me: the feel of firm cotton balls and the touch of velvet fabrics. Both still send shivers up my spine. As I have paid attention to these little touches that displease me, I have eliminated them from our home. Needless to say, you will find no velvet upholstered chairs in my living room, and only soft, fluffy cotton balls in our bathroom canister. Ask your family what textures they enjoy, and then make every effort to incorporate those touches into your home.

Touch Today

Filling our homes with comfortable things today should come easily. All we need do is open our eyes, turn on our feelers to what is around, and take notice of what soothes and satisfies us. We are bombarded with choices for comfort. Linen stores overflow with lovely towels, sheets, rugs, and comforters. Furniture stores are filled with upholstery pieces to suit every seating preference possible. We can buy mattresses in the size and firmness we desire, rugs and carpets in many textures and styles, and sofas and chairs to suit our seating preferences. By paying attention to each little detail of touch, we will be making our homes more pleasant places in which to live.

"Houses that express comfort and well-being can go a long way toward making us feel at home in the world."
— JoAnn Barwick

COMFORTING ENTRANCES

The first step inside our homes should bring us comfort and contentment. Though we have little control over the harsh realities of the outside world, we can do much to bring tender touch inside. Creating a comfortable atmosphere in the entrances to our homes can immediately convey a sense of safety, security, and great satisfaction.

The First Step

Begin making your entrance comfortable with a pretty area rug inside your front and back doors. This will be the first touch of comfort family and friends experience as they step into your home. Choose a colorful cotton rag rug, an oval braided rug, or a homey hook rug with a playful pattern. I have a dear friend whose front hallway holds a hook rug and runner overflowing with flowers and bunnies. These warm touches fill her entrance with comfort and charm.

Select entrance rugs that are not only pretty, but practical. Try to find ones with a medium-color background or plenty of pattern that will camouflage dirt tracked in from outside. To prolong the life of your rug and prevent slipping, use a vinyl mesh grip beneath it.

I helped decorate a friend's home, and it had become quite comfortable. But her two-story front entrance, though furnished, still seemed stark. In an effort to cozy it up before a Christmas party, we bought two beautiful 5 x 7 rugs. As soon as we rolled them out, her entrance instantly became warm and welcoming. The rugs brought colorful comfort and the finishing touch to her entrance, and tied the adjacent rooms together beautifully. When the guests arrived, their first step inside was comforting.

Homecoming Hugs and Kisses

Life is so short. Whether it's been a month, a week, a day, or just a few hours, seeing a loved one step safely back home should be a cherished ritual. A cheerful homecoming communicates to a family member, "Your presence around here matters! You are important! You were missed! You are special! You are loved!"

"Comfort is a room you love being in without knowing why."
— Paul Leonard

At our house, coming home is cause for celebration. No matter who's at home or who's coming home, when the garage door opener sounds or the back door swings open, it's the signal for whomever is home (even our dog, Ruff) to stop everything and run to the door for a warm greeting of hugs and kisses (and lots of licks!). If I'm home and talking on the phone, I try to end the conversation. If I'm cooking, I turn off the stove. If I've been out working on a design job or running errands, I make every effort to get home to hug Bill as he walks through the door. It may not always be convenient, but the joy I get from kissing his smiling face, eager to be welcomed home, is well worth the sacrifice.

I realize that in many cases it may not be possible for you to be home when family members arrive. If you can't be there to give them a physical touch and a personal greeting, leave them a written touch. In a note, tell them where you are and when you'll be home.

This thoughtful gesture gives a sense of love and security to anyone entering an empty home.

But when you *can* be home, are you? And when you are home, do you greet your family with a grunt and a groan as you're going about your business, or do you take the time to warmly meet each one with your tender, loving touch? How rude we would find it if, when visiting someone's home, they didn't greet us at the door and give us a warm welcome? Certainly, our loved ones deserve the same consideration and kindness we would extend to others.

In her book *Open Heart, Open Home*, Karen Mains speaks heartily about the importance of the homecoming, " ... it is often an accurate thermometer which gauges what we truly feel toward our house mates. I suspect that the quality of our front door reception can greatly determine the atmosphere of that afternoon and evening's life together." I guarantee that if you make your entrance a comforting place of welcoming touch, your family will always be eager to head home.

If you grew up in a home where positive touch was freely given, you are probably very comfortable touching others. However, if you were raised in a home where touch was not an important ingredient, expressing love by touching others may be very difficult for you. It's not too late to change. If you feel paralyzed when it comes to touching, stretch yourself by reaching out to someone you love. Like anything in life, the more you do it, the easier it becomes. In time, touching can be a very natural part of your life and will bless the ones you touch, as well as yourself.

We all have different levels of comfort when it comes to touch, but none can deny the scientific results that indicate a healthier, happier life for those who experience frequent, loving touch. According to a *USA Today* article, "Physical affection and warmth towards kids strongly predicted closer marriages and friendships ... better mental health and more work success." Jo Lindberg, founder of the Hugs for Health Foundation confirms, "Hugs are the best form of emotional and physical therapy." It seems that welcoming our loved ones home with hugs can do more than simply make their day.

If you live alone, or if you simply love animals, find a furry friend to greet you at your entrance door. Our fluffy, white bichon frise, Ruff, is always waiting eagerly by our back door for his touch

"Make home a happy place they look forward to coming back to."
— Ruth Bell Graham

of love. I have to admit, I love to touch him too. As humans, we could benefit from observing the behavior of our pets. They are not afraid or ashamed to let us know they want to be touched.

Blessed with Guests

When guests visit your home, make their time a rich blessing they will remember. In welcoming a friend to your home, give him or her a warm hug or a friendly, firm handshake. For an extra touch of sincerity and love, give a double-handed handshake. When someone greets me this way, I sense a genuine spirit and a big heart. Any thoughtful gesture of touch instantly conveys love and acceptance and puts others at ease when entering your home.

Have a guest book and pen displayed on a table or chest by your front door. Select a book that coordinates with your decorating scheme. As friends or relatives are departing, invite them to leave their personal touch in your home by signing your guest book. It will take just a moment, but the memories will last for years. I love to flip through our guest book and reminisce over special relationships celebrated in the comfort of our home. Our little guest book holds memories of special moments I might otherwise have forgotten. If you have a friend moving into a new home, consider a beautiful guest book as a thoughtful housewarming gift.

"I never like the giving of a hand, unless the entire body accompanies it!"
— Ralph Waldo Emerson

❖

COMFORTING LIVING ROOMS

For me, a living room is successful only when it is comfortable. If it is comfortable, then it is livable. There is nothing more awkward or uninviting than walking into a picture perfect living room where the furniture seems to say "Don't sit on me," and the accessories shout "Don't touch me!" A room like that is not a living room; it's a showroom. A comfortable living room is an inviting place that welcomes you with the open arms of not only its owners, but its contents. It begs you to sit on the tousled sofa. It hopes you will open the well-worn photo album filled with pictures of family and friends. It invites you to curl up under the cozy cotton throw.

A comforting living room evolves as we pay attention to the little details. Our living rooms, as well as our entire homes, are filled with things. The more attuned we are to what things satisfy our sense of touch, the more we can integrate into our living rooms those textures that appeal to us and eliminate those that don't.

Furniture Placement

Warmth and intimacy in your living room can be achieved in great part through the placement of your furnishings. Though you may not physically touch those with whom you are sitting and talking, it is important that your hearts and souls touch, and this can happen only when your furnishings are placed properly. Furniture arrangement communicates much like body language. When someone stands close with open arms, you know they are at ease and accept you. Likewise, when furnishings are placed purposely in close proximity, they will add warmth and emotional connection with the people in the room. Such an arrangement is far more intimate and inviting than seating that is spread out over a large area with huge gaps of space in between. If you have a large room, consider creating two smaller sitting areas to avoid this problem.

Furniture arrangement communicates much like body language.

As you consider how to place your furniture, think about your lifestyle. Will the furniture be arranged around a focal point? How many people do you need to seat comfortably? What type of seating do you prefer? Do you need to add flexible seating for guests? All of these choices will affect how your furniture should be placed. Decide how your furniture will be arranged before making any major upholstery purchases. You may love the look and comfort of a huge chair and a half, but it may not fit properly in your living room.

Selecting a Sofa

The seating you choose greatly affects your living room's degree of comfort, intimacy, and pleasure. One of the largest and most important pieces of furniture in the living room is the sofa. A comfortable sofa can make a big difference in how often you, your family, and friends occupy your living room. If you are just beginning to create a comforting living room, a sofa is an excellent starting point.

Since a sofa can be a fairly expensive purchase, really think about what you want in a sofa before you buy one. Years ago, Bill and I made a poor purchase. I blew it. I fell in love with an over-stuffed sofa that looked dreamy in the furniture store. It had rolled arms, big bun feet, and was covered in a crisp blue and white awning stripe canvas fabric. The price was right. The look was great. I pleaded and begged Bill for it, convinced him of what a find it was, and got my way. We bought it and had it delivered.

A great deal is no deal at all if it is not comfortable.

Just as I thought, the sofa looked great in our living room. But, in buying on a whim, what I failed to consider carefully was its comfort. The sofa has lots of loose cushions stacked across the back that we can never manage to get quite comfortable. The result is that we seldom sit on it. It's like buying a pair of shoes on sale that look great but don't feel great, so you never wear them. Lesson learned: A great deal is no deal at all if it is not comfortable. No doubt, experience is the best teacher. Whatever type of sofa you choose for your living room, comfort should be a key consideration.

If you are in the market for a new sofa, save your pennies and splurge on one that is well-made and comfortable. It will bring you pleasure for years to come. Before you buy it, have all of your family sit on it to make sure it's a fit. Check the seat height and depth and arm height. The best quality coil construction for a sofa is one that is eight-way hand-tied. The coils are literally tied by hand in eight different directions and therefore very supportive. Most leading manufacturers use this type of construction, but be sure to ask. Sofas that are well-constructed can be given new life simply by being reupholstered or slipcovered.

The type of cushion filling you choose contributes greatly to the comfort and look of your sofa. Your main considerations in cushion comfort are firmness and maintenance. How far do you want to sink, and how often do you want to fluff? Cushions can be foam, spring with fiber-fill, spring-down, or down. Foam and fiber-fill are the firmest, least expensive, and retain their shape the best. However, these cushions offer less "give" to conform to your body.

Spring-down cushions are made with coil springs surrounded by down feathers. A spring-down cushion retains most of its shape.

This is probably the best cushion if you like a somewhat plush seat, but don't want to be constantly fluffing cushions.

Down cushions are the ultimate in luxury. You don't sit on down cushions; you sink into them. The cushions curl up around you, tempting you to never get up. But the cushions don't retain their shape, and must be fluffed often to keep their comfortable, plush feel. I'm partial to the comfort of down cushions. I like the tousled look of cushions that are indented where someone sat before me. It shows the living room is really lived in, and that makes me feel comfortable and at home.

The fabric you choose to cover your sofa in also affects its comfort. When selecting fabrics, choose them for their feel, as well as their look. Try a nubbly wool, woven muslin, textured damask, slippery chintz, or sturdy denim. Textured fabrics can add interest and pleasant touch to any upholstered furniture, but especially a large, frequently used piece like a living room sofa. Generally, the more textured and heavier a fabric is to the touch, the tougher and more durable it will be on your sofa. Whatever fabric you select for your upholstered furniture, make sure it is practical and pleasing to your touch in addition to being pleasing to your eye.

The more comfortable we are, the more content we are.

Chairs that Comfort

Cozy chairs can contribute to creating a comforting living room too. Their quality construction requirements are similar to that of a sofa. A favorite chair should suit your personality and lifestyle and soothe your body and mind every time you sit in it. You may prefer an overstuffed club chair, a gliding wooden rocker, a wide wing chair, or a stretching recliner.

My most cherished and comfortable chair in our home is a lovely floral chintz Louis XV chair that belonged to Bill's grandmother, Lalla. The chair, which now sits gracefully by a sunny window, is a treasured antique that holds a lifetime of family memories. I have many reasons to love this chair, but above all, I love it primarily for the plush, down seat cushion into which I adore sinking. It's not only my favorite place to sit; it's Ruff's favorite too. He's not a dumb dog — he knows comfort when he feels it!

If there's a man in your home, a great way to love, honor, and respect him is by designating a comfortable throne he can call his own. My father-in-law has a recliner he loves dearly. There is no other place on earth he would rather sit. It's where he feels at home, because it is comfortable to his body and familiar to his touch. We have many special memories of family gatherings in the Willits' living room. The adults and children may be scattered about, but Bill's father can always be found in the center of activity, proudly perched in his favorite recliner.

"Love and faithfulness keep a king safe; through love his throne is made secure."
— Proverbs 20:28

Flexible Furniture

When I help clients make purchase decisions on upholstered furniture, I highly recommend adding a swivel base to a club chair for greater flexibility and enjoyment. This simple feature gives the freedom to swing one way and watch a roaring fire or twirl around and take part in a conversation. The slight additional cost to add a swivel base will be well worth the added comfort and convenience.

Another excellent way to add comfort and versatility to your living room is with an ottoman. An ottoman can be large or small; round, square, or rectangular; tufted, tasseled, or ruffled — whatever suits your room and your touch. An ottoman should be at least one inch lower than the seat height of a sofa or chair and should have casters so it can be moved easily around the room. It can function as a handy foot rest to prop up tired legs, as an extra seat when needed, or as a convenient place in the center of your conversation area to display a stack of beautiful books or accommodate a serving tray. Large ottomans covered in durable fabrics or leather serve as wonderful coffee tables. They're practical, multifunctional, and, unlike a wood or glass-top table, they welcome you to put your feet up.

We have a large rectangular ottoman in front of the loveseat in our study. Both the loveseat and ottoman are covered in a cranberry red and forest green cotton plaid. The jumbo ottoman makes the loveseat feel like a double recliner. For a cozy evening, we use it to hold a dinner or snack tray. We sit with our feet up, cuddle under a warm blanket, and watch a movie. When we need additional seating, we move the ottoman to an appropriate spot.

Pillow Talk

Floor pillows are a fun way to add flexible seating to your living room. I love to stack two or three jumbo, twenty-four-inch or larger square pillows on the floor or prop them up against a sofa. Floor pillows are relatively inexpensive compared to other pieces of furniture, yet they serve as a great support for someone who wants to plop on the floor to watch a movie or sit in front of a flaming fire. Whenever we have a roomful of friends over for a casual get-together, the most sought-out sitting spot is among the jumbo pillows spread out on the living room floor. I always encourage clients to take advantage of floor pillows. They're comfortable, safe, and practical. Kids love them! Load up your living room, play room, or children's bedrooms with floor pillows. With zippered coverings, they are easy to clean and less costly to replace than upholstered furniture.

"Comfort is perhaps the ultimate luxury."
— Billy Baldwin

Make your sofa, chairs, and benches extra comfortable by tossing on a few plump, plush pillows. They come in a variety of sizes, shapes, and contents that all lend a touch of comfort. Fiber-filled pillow forms work well for decorative pillows. They are inexpensive, nonallergenic, and retain their shape. But for the ultimate touch of luxury, use down-filled pillows. The comfortable down filling will conform to your body for a cozy backrest.

Comfortable Floors

The flooring in our living rooms needs to be comfortable, durable, and practical. Possibilities for floor coverings are endless, but carpet is the type most often used, because of its affordability and comfort. When selecting carpet, think comfort and quality first, then color. Walk on it with your bare feet to be sure it is soft. For high traffic areas like living rooms, choose a durable, dense pile, tight-level or cut-loop carpet. Berber carpet is a good choice for any busy area. Its tight-level loop and neutral tone make it extremely durable. However, it is important to have Berber installed by a knowledgeable carpet installer to assure seams are properly concealed. For lower traffic areas, like bedrooms, deeper, plush piles can be used, though I prefer to use the same carpet throughout a home for continuity.

The quality of padding used is equally important to the durability of your carpet. Buy the best padding you can afford. Like a box spring for a mattress, the padding provides support for your carpet. Though the purpose of carpet padding is to absorb foot traffic and reduce carpet wear and stretching, it enhances comfort as well.

Hard surface flooring, though more costly than carpet, is a lovely way to bring texture and interest to your living room. Hardwood floors, terra cotta tiles, stone, slate, or brick are among the many natural resources God created that can be used to enhance our homes. Wood floors are the most popular hard surface flooring.

When possible, use a variety of natural materials to bring comfort and beauty to your living room. The home in which I grew up had gray slate throughout the living room and kitchen floors. The fireplace was laid with old bricks, and the walls were paneled in knotty pine. The varied natural finishes brought a great deal of charm and warmth to the room where much of our family time was spent.

If your room has hard surface flooring, consider using area rugs to add comfort and interest. Try a dhurrie, Oriental, Persian, or needlepoint rug to frame a cozy conversation area. Rugs can also be laid on top of carpet to define a space. Lay rugs in major traffic areas to protect hard surface floors and soften the step.

When we were renovating our home, we had a fixed budget, as most people do. We so wanted hardwoods in our main living area for their look, but mostly for their durability and easy care. Bill and I, along with several incredible friends and family members, did much of the interior painting to save money so we could swing the hardwoods. The exhausting paint job is almost forgotten, but the enjoyment of our beautiful hardwood floors will last for years.

We were blessed to inherit several Oriental rugs that once covered the floors of Bill's grandparents' home. In the cooler months, I roll out these treasures onto our hardwood floors and our casual living room is filled with both beauty to please the eyes and comfort to please our toes.

In the warmer months, or for a casual look anytime, use natural fiber rugs, like sisal or seagrass. With their neutral-colored textured weave, these practical rugs subtly enhance any room with hard surface flooring. Before purchasing a natural fiber rug, walk on it with

A comfortable home is an inviting place that welcomes you with the open arms of not only its people, but its contents.

your bare feet. Some are more comfortable than others. I am especially fond of the touch and texture of seagrass. A client of mine wanted to cover a portion of her newly refinished hardwood living room floors, yet her budget was limited. The casual, comfortable, and reasonably-priced seagrass was the perfect choice. The natural fiber hides dirt, is smooth to walk on, and has a foam backing to protect floors, provide cushion, and prevent slipping.

Pleasant Paperwork

Paperwork is unavoidable. But as long as you must tend to it, why not make it as pleasant as possible? Whether you pay bills, read mail, or write letters in a cozy corner of your living room or a separate office, simple little touches can enhance the job.

Make opening mail a pleasant ritual. At a quiet moment during your day, sit down and unveil your mail using a pretty letter opener. A letter opener will not only add beauty to the task, but it will also spare your hand and nails. We were given a lovely, crystal handled letter knife years ago. I keep it close at hand and treasure its touch as I open our mail.

Once you have opened your mail, immediately dispose of the unimportant items in a decorative trash can beside your desk. Then find an attractive way to display that which needs your attention. Paperwork stashed away in a desk drawer is too easily forgotten — out of sight, out of touch, out of mind! Brass letter racks, silver toast caddies, or baskets can all be used for filing correspondence, paying bills, and responding to invitations. A flat basket on my desk holds my necessary paperwork.

Make filing your paperwork enjoyable by organizing your folders in an efficient and attractive manner. For easy reference, color coordinate your file folders according to different topics: personal, business, household, etc. My green files are for my interior design business; they hold all my client information and documentation. Yellow, my favorite color, is for personal papers, like medical, dental, and household records. Red files the passion of my heart, my writing resources. A cheerful friend of mine, Shelby Bosse, organizes all her files in purple and red folders. Pick colors you prefer and have fun getting your filing life in order.

"Whatever your hand finds to do, do it with all your might . . ."
— Ecclesiastes 9:10

Keep invitations to remind you to jot a quick thank-you note as soon as you have attended the event. Many people today fail to extend their gratefulness or love to others in the form of a note or letter, perhaps because life seems too busy and the effort to gather the needed writing equipment too time-consuming. Scripture tells us in 1 Thessalonians 5:11 to "encourage one another" and in verse 18, "to give thanks in all circumstances." One way we can encourage others and demonstrate a grateful heart is with a note of thanks.

God gave us our hands not only for laboring, but for loving.

To make keeping in touch with others a pleasure, fill a compartmented basket with your favorite stationery, note cards, post cards, roll of stamps, letter opener, address book, and a pen you enjoy using. The more convenient note writing is, the more likely you are to keep in touch and the more lives you can bless. Even if your life is busy, you can minister from your home through the mail.

One of the women who has had the most profound spiritual influence in my life has done so primarily by writing me encouraging letters. She has a busy life, but it is fruitful, partly because she knows the value of encouraging others with her written word.

The greatest blessing of any note or letter is that it lasts. I keep special notes and letters stored in a decorative yellow hat box I call my "sunshine box." On a rainy, blue day when my spirits need a lift, I pull them out to read.

Happy Hands

God gave us our hands in part for laboring. We are told in Proverbs 31:13 of the godly woman who worked "with eager hands." When we make the labor we do in our homes more enjoyable, our hands are apt to be more eager to work.

When it comes to dusting your living room furniture, or any wood furniture, throw out those scrimpy scraps of miscellaneous torn T-shirts and tattered towels commonly used for dusting. Instead, buy a dozen cotton diapers to dust your furniture. They will be soft to your touch and attract dust like a magnet, without leaving lint behind. Wash them after each use, and store them in a pretty basket. For hard-to-reach places, use an ostrich feather duster. Rather than viewing dusting as a drag, make it a pleasant time of touch to care for your things and thank God for his provisions.

Polish brass, glass, copper, and silver with quality cleaners, paper towels, and sponges. Cleaning and caring for that which we have is simply being a good steward of what God has entrusted to us. I love polishing favorite objects like our silver bell, given as a wedding favor. Restoring its natural beauty gives me a sense of satisfaction and reminds me of our brother and sister-in-law's marriage celebration.

Whether you like hand hobbies such as cross-stitching, knitting, or needlepoint or you're like me and simply sew on a button now and then, have a pretty sewing basket to make such jobs a joy. Fill it with the necessary ingredients: threads, yarns, pins, needles, sharp scissors, and a thimble. Keep your basket close at hand in your living room for whenever you have the itch to sit and work with eager hands. The more convenient it is, the more you'll be apt to do it.

"The homeliest tasks get beautiful if loving hands do them."
— Louisa May Alcott

COMFORTING KITCHENS

There is no room in the home where our hands labor more than in our kitchens. From pouring that first cup of morning coffee to drying the last dinner dish, the touch of our hands is required. As we integrate kitchen touches that bring pleasure and convenience, our time and tasks in this room will become more enjoyable.

Helping Hands

Putting on a pretty apron is the first step towards creating a comforting kitchen atmosphere. This simple act will prepare your heart and mind, and change what might be considered a burden into a blessing. Just as putting on a tennis skirt helps me feel more like an avid tennis player, tying on an apron somehow makes me feel more qualified for the kitchen tasks before me.

Be sure to take good care of the hands God has given you. When washing dishes, wear rubber gloves to protect your hands and nails. Keep a decorative dispenser filled with your favorite hand lotion by the kitchen sink and apply it frequently. Massaging your hands gently with lotion can be a small reward of touch after laboring to prepare and clean up a meal.

When was the last time you replaced your dish towels and pot holders? Though they cost very little, replacements for items we often use can bring enormous pleasure. It's the little joys in life that give us a lift! Replenish your supply of kitchen towels and hot pads when they become stained or dingy. Buy all-cotton, absorbent dish towels. Drape one over a kitchen cabinet door or thread one through your refrigerator door handle. I love my Williams Sonoma cotton dish towels. They are soft, quite reasonably priced, and come in white with a center stripe of red, yellow, green, or blue. Once a year, I stock up on a fresh supply of white and green ones — a simple touch that helps make my kitchen comfortable.

Another convenient touch is to keep a handy basket next to your kitchen telephone with a notepad and reliable pen to jot down messages and reminders. Try to always leave a note if you must be away from home before someone else is expected to arrive; it's courteous, thoughtful, and will give a sense of security and love to those entering an empty home. Some of my times cooking and cleaning up in the kitchen have been my greatest moments of inspiration for writing ideas. Having paper and pen close by in my kitchen wall basket allows me to write down my thoughts before I forget them and am on to the next thing.

Enjoyable Equipment

Kitchen chores need not be a chore. Sort through your cooking utensils and equipment and keep only those items that work easily and are pleasing to your touch. Whether you prefer a manual or electric can opener, make sure it is dependable and works with ease. For the past year, I have needed to replace my manual can opener but never made it a priority. Every time I reached in the drawer for it to open a can, I dreaded the job before me. I recently made a list of all the unpleasant touches in my kitchen, and the can opener topped the chart. I've now replaced this simple piece of equipment and actually enjoy opening a can. Little touches go a long way!

Are your pots and pans pleasing to your touch? I prefer cooking equipment that is easy to clean and fairly lightweight. Not long ago, I gave away my whole set of iron skillets. I never reached for them because they were heavy to lift and a nuisance to clean. Notice what you enjoy and slowly weed out what you never reach for in your kitchen. The beauty of creating a comforting kitchen is that you can fill yours with items pleasing to your very own touch.

When it's time to cut something, do you hesitate before picking up a knife? Some of the most often used utensils in the kitchen are knives. Knives come in a variety of sizes and shapes, each designed to best handle a specific task. Choosing the right knife can help make any cutting job a pleasure. A large, wide chef's knife is used primarily for mincing, chopping, and slicing fruits and vegetables. A narrower, long, slicing knife with a smooth-edged blade cuts thin, even slices of meats, cheeses, and vegetables. A knife with a serrated edge slices breads and cakes. The medium-size utility or boning knife peels, slices, chops, or removes skin or meat from its bone. The paring knife fits snugly in the hand for small cutting jobs. The knives I most frequently use are my chef's and utility knives. Next time you reach for a knife, make sure you're making your cutting job as easy as it can be by selecting the proper one.

As often as we use our knives, keeping them sharp is important. Ecclesiastes 10:10 says, "If the ax is dull and its edge unsharpened, more strength is needed . . ." Why make food preparation harder than it has to be? Sharpen your knives and scissors when you notice they are dull. At least once a year, I wrap up my knives and take them to a shop to have them professionally sharpened. Check your yellow pages for a sharpening resource. The little effort it takes to have your knives sharpened will save you time in the long run.

Carving a roast or turkey should be part of a celebration, not a needless frustration. To assure this, have a sharp carving knife and serving fork. When cutting with a sharp knife, use a sturdy wood cutting board or butcher's block to protect your counters, handle the knife's pressure, and adequately hold the food you're cutting.

For effortless carving, use a sharp electric knife. Several years ago, we were celebrating Thanksgiving with relatives in a cabin equipped only with the bare basics (one of which was *not* a sharp carving knife). Though our turkey tasted wonderful, by the time it made it off the bone onto the platter, the meat was mutilated — not to mention the fact that, when he was finally done carving, the carver was not in a very thankful mood for the feast before us!

"If the ax is dull and its edge unsharpened, more strength is needed . . ."
— Ecclesiastes 10:10

Convenient Cleanup

Emptying the kitchen trash is often a dreaded chore, no matter who does it. Make it as easy as possible by lining a large decorative trash can with a sturdy garbage bag with built-in drawstrings. Store additional bags in the bottom of your trash can. No more fumbling with your fingers to find those ties, twisties, or replacement bags.

You can make your dirty sponges look and feel like new again by washing them in your dishwasher. Before I learned this simple touch, I used to put my dirty sponges in the washing machine. Though they would come out clean, they were destroyed, bit by bit, in the vigorous wash cycle.

Don't skimp on the quality of paper towel you buy for your kitchen. The better quality the paper product, the less you will need. Find and stick with a brand that has a nice feel and good absorbency. Use coupons, and stock up on your paper towel when you see it on sale. I prefer purchasing the extra large rolls to save time and energy replacing them.

COMFORTING DINING ROOMS

The most enjoyable dining experiences are those that exude comfort with every touch. From the seat we take to the napkin we grasp to the glass we lift, each simple detail can stimulate our sense of touch to make savoring a meal all the more satisfying.

Hospitality Hints

Nothing warms my heart more than to be at a table of family and friends and have the host or hostess stretch out their hands to those beside them before giving God thanks. It says to me, "We are family." Try to make it a special ritual in your home to hold hands while giving thanks at meals or anytime you pray with others. Give an extra "I love you" squeeze at the end of the prayer. Don't underestimate the power of hand-holding. Over one-third of our five million touch receptors are in our hands. The simple act of hand-holding can knit hearts and lives together.

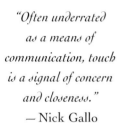

"Often underrated as a means of communication, touch is a signal of concern and closeness."
— Nick Gallo

After praying, most people reach for their napkins. What a perfect time for a touch of surprise! To enhance a pretty place setting, add some flair to your napkin folding. Folded napkins are an easy way to bring a touch of life and love to your table. Buy a book on napkin folding and learn a few, simple folds. Wrap decorative rings, ribbon, or a simple strand of raffia around your napkins for a touch of interest. Clip clothespins to checked napkins for a casual picnic feel. Thread a lacy napkin through a delicate tea cup handle for a dainty touch. Twist the center of a fluffy napkin and stuff it in a pretty stemmed glass. Though I don't like to fuss when it comes to setting my table, I do like my napkins to have a touch of creativity. For a quick trick, I often tie a fabric napkin into a loose knot in the center to make it look like a bow.

We use white terry cloth hand towels as napkins almost every day in our home. I keep a clean supply in a basket by our kitchen table. Terry cloth napkins are tender to the touch and absorbent; they're also economical and easy to care for. You can wash and bleach them clean, toss them in the dryer, and they don't need ironing.

For an extra special touch after feasting on messy finger foods, dampen your hand towels with water, roll them up, and warm them in the microwave for thirty seconds. Your family and friends will feel like royalty. So little effort . . . so much enjoyment!

Though I much prefer the feel of a fabric napkin, I will use paper ones, in an instant, if it means I don't have to iron. Paper napkins come in beverage, luncheon, and dinner sizes. Stock up on colorful ones that look pretty in your home to enhance any meal or beverage. Don't just save them for visitors — for a touch of love, treat your family and yourself to pretty paper napkins. When serving a beverage, offer a small decorative paper napkin or coaster as a gracious gesture of touch. It will make the beverage easier to hold if it is extremely hot or cold, and will protect your furniture as well.

The simple act of hand-holding can knit hearts and lives together.

A Soft Seat

Make sure your dining chair seats are as comfortable as possible. If you have wood chairs, cover them with soft seat cushions and accessorize with ties, tassels, or tufting. A cushion brings beauty and comfort as it softens the seat. To prevent chair pads from slipping and sliding while you sit on them, simply cut inexpensive rug grip into several pieces and place a piece underneath each chair pad.

If you have a bay window in your dining area, enjoy it all the more by making it a cozy, comfortable window seat. Adding hinges to your window seat lid will allow you to use the space below for storage. Make a seat cushion for the window seat out of a practical and pretty fabric and pile on the pillows; it will become a favorite spot for not only eating, but for curling up with a good book or simply daydreaming out the window.

A hug loves, but a hold heals.

A Tasty Touch

When you reach in your cabinet for a glass or cup to pour a beverage, do you always grab the same old thing? If you have several different types of glassware, take them out and use them! Select an appropriate beverage glass to enhance your touch and sipping satisfaction. I like to serve sweet iced tea in a wide-mouth mason jar, steamy coffee in a chunky mug, and hot tea in a delicate teacup.

I keep several casual stemmed glasses in our freezer. When I want to serve fresh fruit juice or any cold beverage, I pull them out for instantly chilled, frosty glasses. My visitors always remark on this special little touch.

You can use the same idea when serving salads or cold desserts by chilling plates or bowls in your freezer. Because my father worked in the hotel and restaurant business throughout my childhood, we were blessed to occasionally dine at lovely restaurants, even as young children. One of our family's favorite restaurants was a fancy Italian restaurant called Capriccio. Every time the waiter served our crisp salad on chilled glass plates, I would touch my cold plate and think myself quite grown-up to be enjoying such a luxury.

Complement the temperature of hot foods as well by heating glass plates and the bowl the food will go into. Simply place plates in a warm oven for a few minutes before dishing up food. (Don't forget to use hot pads when you serve them!) This is an especially pleasing touch in the chill of winter.

The temperature of any food greatly enhances the enjoyment it brings. Be sure to serve cold foods cold and hot foods hot. Bill loves his hot food piping hot, so I always try to make sure to serve it that way. I may have to microwave his meal for a few seconds to get it to the temperature he desires, but the extra effort is well worth seeing the smile on his face as he inhales the steamy, hot vapor rising from his plate of food.

Comforting Bedrooms

Because our bedrooms are the rooms to which we retire for rest and renewal, they must be comforting to our touch — perhaps more so than any other room in our homes. Like a bird gathers natural things and weaves them into her nest to create a place of warmth, security, and comfort, so we can feather our bedrooms by gathering comfortable, lovely materials that are pleasing to the touch.

Beauty draws you in, but comfort keeps you there.

Satisfying Sleep

There's nothing like a good night's sleep in your own bed to get the rest you need. Most of us spend over thirty percent of our lives in bed, so it is essential that every bit of our bedding be comfortable.

The first step in making your bed comfortable is to have an excellent mattress as its foundation. Since we use a bed more than any other piece of furniture, having a quality mattress is one of the wisest investments we can make to bring comfort to our homes. The average person moves about fifty times in a single night. With all that movement, a supportive mattress will cradle you comfortably, allowing you to sleep deeply and feel refreshed for the next day.

The construction of your mattress set is very important to your sleeping comfort. If your mattress surface appears uneven, creaks, or shakes when you roll over, or if you wake up with aches and pains, you probably need a new mattress set. Before you purchase a mattress, lie down on several to determine which feels best to you. The firmness you select depends on your personal preference. A good quality mattress should last ten years. Be sure to buy a matching box spring when purchasing a mattress. The two are engineered to work together to provide maximum comfort and durability. If you share your bed with a mate, a queen- or king-size bed is a must to provide the needed sleeping space. If, however, you have different firmness needs, buy two twin mattresses and attach them together with king sheets. Both of your sleeping needs are equally important for a pleasant home atmosphere.

When I worked at Weir's Furniture Store in Dallas, I had the privilege of helping one of the owners, Patsy Moore, redecorate her home. In gratitude, she told me to select any piece of furniture I wanted from the store. I felt like a kid in a candy shop! After visualizing every beautiful piece of furniture in our home, we finally settled on a deluxe, extra-firm, pillow-top mattress. It may have been terribly practical and certainly not as beautiful as a mahogany poster bed, but it has given us more comfort than any other piece of furniture we own. We didn't realize how uncomfortable our old mattress was until we experienced a truly good night's sleep on our new one.

Once you've purchased a quality mattress, maintain it properly by flipping it every month. This will ensure that it wears better, stays comfortable, and lasts as long as possible. Another way to maintain your mattress is with a quality mattress cover. Use a thick, quilted mattress cover to add a layer of softness between the satiny mattress top and your bottom sheet and to protect your mattress from moisture. Mattress covers are available in many textures and materials.

Envelope your mattress and mattress cover in bedsheets that are beautiful, comfortable, and pleasing to your touch. Cool cotton sheets will soothe you in the summer. Cozy flannel sheets will warm you in the winter. And silky satin sheets add a little luxury anytime. The finest-quality sheets are all-cotton and have high thread counts. Most all-cotton sheets today are treated so they don't need ironing. Other no-iron sheets are those blended with polyester. Though less expensive, the polyester blends feel coarser than all-cotton sheets and tend to pill after excessive wear. Despite the endless array of beautiful decorative sheets available today, I still prefer the simplicity and purity of white all-cotton sheets. They are cool, crisp, and clean with any decorating scheme and can easily be bleached to keep them pure white.

A Comforting Cover-Up

Young or old, curling up under a cozy blanket gives a sense of security. Lay a mohair or cashmere throw or a cotton or wool blanket at the foot of your bed. It will be within easy reach for extra warmth at night or to snuggle under during an afternoon nap. For an extra touch, layer your bed blanket between two flat sheets. The top sheet will keep your blanket clean and be smooth and soft to the touch.

Choose a blanket not only for its color and content, but its texture. Natural wool blankets for example, are the warmest, though quite expensive and sometimes scratchy. Acrylic blankets are an economical alternative to wool. Many people enjoy the warmth of an acrylic electric blanket during the winter. The temperature of an electric blanket is adjustable on both sides to easily satisfy two temperature preferences. I prefer the feel and warmth of natural blankets to that of an electric or acrylic blanket. I especially enjoy the comforting feel of cotton thermal blankets that have an open weave.

Quilts are a lovely and long-lasting way to bring the color and comfort of cotton to your home. Collect pretty quilts that coordinate with your decor. Often used as a coverlet, quilts can also be folded at the end of your bed, over a chest, hung on a wall, or draped over a table and covered with glass. When decorating a client's mountain home, we used beautiful handmade quilts as our starting point for each bedroom. My grandmother's handmade tufted quilt is folded at the end of our bed. It's a treasured heirloom that I love, and it's wonderfully comfortable. We take it with us on trips in the car for a little touch of home.

Another way to cover yourself up is with a goose down or duvet comforter. A duvet is lightweight and cool in the summer and warm in the winter. It is the European cousin to our American coverlets and can replace the bedspread and blanket as well as the traditional top sheet. With a duvet, making the bed is a breeze! All you do is "duvet" or "fluff" and smooth the comforter. It's an easy way for young children to learn to make their beds.

I first discovered the luxury of a duvet while traveling with friends in Europe after graduating from college. We were staying in a quaint inn at the foot of the beautiful Matterhorn in Zermatt, Switzerland. The nights were quite cold, but crawling under my duvet was like nestling under a huge pile of fluffy clouds. I still remember the comfort of those nights. I have such fond memories of

"It's a delicious moment, certainly, that of being well nestled in bed and feeling that you shall drop gently to sleep . . ."

— Leigh Hunt

185

it that now Bill and I have treated ourselves to a duvet on our bed that we enjoy year-round. It makes for sweet dreams.

Plush Pillows

*A clean conscience is
a soft pillow.*

Have you ever thought about the kind of pillow you prefer? It may seem silly, but your choice of pillows can make a big difference in the comfort of your home. For years, I have battled neck and back aches. In desperation for some relief, I decided to try a therapeutic pillow. It is made of a firm, contoured foam that cradles my neck. When I sleep on my special pillow, the physical aches and pains go away. Bill, however, prefers the softness of down pillows, so our bed is piled high with lots of different pillows pleasing to our different touch preferences.

Bed pillows come in many materials: foam, poly-fill, down, and down and feathers. They are available in several sizes: king, queen, standard, and even body size. Decide which size and texture you prefer, and don't feel limited to a certain size just because it's your bed size. We have a king bed but sleep with standard size pillows. Their size suits us better.

Let each family member choose which pillow type they prefer. Be picky about your bed pillows. Surround yourself with pillows that give you comfort; after all, a good night's sleep affects your attitude and your home atmosphere. To enhance the life of your pillows and keep them clean, protect them with zip-on cotton covers before slipping them into pillow cases.

Decorative pillows can enhance and soften your bed when it is made. They too come in many different sizes and shapes — square, round, neck rolls, and baby pillows. To create an irresistibly inviting bed, use a variety. A friend of mine, Pam Kuester, told me that her husband, Jeff, had asked while they were making their bed one morning, whether all the pillows were really necessary. She replied, "Only if we want our bed to be beautiful." I wholeheartedly agree — the more pillows, the better!

If you sit up in bed and read or write (as I do), or enjoy watching television there, a decorative pillow with arms and a firm back can help prop you. A neck-roll pillow tucked behind several stacked bed pillows can also provide lower back support. A pillow prop can become a favorite form of bedroom comfort.

Rest In Peace

One final note about the soothing touch of our beds. We need to make them comfortable. We need to make them beautiful. But most importantly, we need to lie down and use them. I am convinced that a lot of problems in our homes could be solved if people were better rested.

I know that if I am overly tired, I become irritable and my perspective on everything becomes distorted. This attitude affects not only me, but the whole atmosphere of our home. A twenty-minute nap can refresh me and give me a new outlook. If time allows and your body is craving it, give in and take a guilt-free nap. We need to rest when we are weary.

There is a vast difference between laziness and rest. In Patricia Sprinkle's insightful book, *Women Who Do Too Much: Stress and the Myth of the Superwoman*, she points to a study that shows naps can significantly lower stress levels and should be a part of our lifestyle. So if you want to reduce a little stress, and you can sneak in a few minutes, take an occasional nap.

If you have little ones at home or work full-time outside the home, and the reality of a nap is floating somewhere out in "Never Never Land," perhaps a more realistic way for you to get rest is by going to bed earlier. Curling into bed early can be a treat sure to bring a better tomorrow. Whatever it takes, make rest a priority. The proper dose of rest is a vital ingredient in creating a comforting home.

Your Cozy Corner

If space allows, include a small sitting area in your bedroom with a loveseat, chair, and tea table. Homes today provide additional space in the master bedroom for a private sitting area. Here, you can sit alone and read or sit with a loved one for a late snack and a chat. If your bedroom space is tight, consider a chaise lounge or small club chair and ottoman with a petite end table and floor lamp.

Make sure this special spot in your bedroom is cozy, intimate, and well-lighted. Perhaps you'll want to use it as your place to get in

"That we are not much sicker and much madder than we are is due exclusively to that most blessed and blessing of all natural graces, sleep."
— Aldous Huxley

touch and be alone with God. Keep your Bible, devotional book, journal, or whatever you use within easy reach. When cuddled up in your cozy corner, take a few moments to jot in a journal. It's a great tool to keep in touch with your personal thoughts, feelings, and prayers. Journaling helps clear your mind of clutter and see patterns in your life more objectively. It also lets you see God's faithful hand unravel life's challenges.

As a young girl, I treasured writing in my tiny diary that I kept under lock and key. It held my deepest heart's desires, as well as lots of day-to-day things that, at the time, were very important to me.

Today my journal habits continue, but now I use my journaling to talk to my Heavenly Father, filling the pages of my spiral notebook with praises, prayers, disappointments, confessions, and simple conversation with God. It is one of the most important touches in my life.

Though there are several areas in my home to which I like to steal away for a few moments with God, my bed is my favorite place for treasured quiet times. I prop myself up with lots of pillows and curl up under my duvet. This is where I feel most warm, secure, and intimate with the Lord. It is my sanctuary. Find the place that suits you best and visit it often. The more convenient and comfortable your little corner of the world, the more likely you will find yourself there. And you, as well as those with whom you live, will be greatly blessed because of it.

"As a mother comforts her child, so I will comfort you."
— Isaiah 66:13

Comfortable Clothing

We can simplify much of the stress in our lives by simplifying our choices. Comfort should always be a key consideration in what we keep. Make putting on your clothes a pleasure by cleaning out your closet and dresser drawers every spring and fall. Lay all your clothes on your bed. Try each garment on. If it fits and you wear it, keep it. If it needs ironing, mending, or altering, fix it. If you haven't worn it in a year, give it away and allow someone else to enjoy it.

When cleaning out your drawers, consider pitching those pitiful sweat pants and purchasing at least one comfortable, attractive outfit for you to pull on when lounging around the house. Why sacrifice beauty in order to be casual and comfortable? Of all the places you should want to be both casual and attractive, it's in the comfort of your home with your loved ones.

As you sort through your nightwear, get rid of ragged, shrunken, or old pajamas. Have just a few pretty, comfortable pieces of night-wear for each season. Do you like nightgowns or do you prefer paja-mas? Short or long? If you are married, what style does your husband enjoy seeing you in? Select fabrics made of all-cotton, flan-nel, silk, rayon, or satin. Natural fabrics are more enjoyable because they allow your skin to breathe. Buy and wear nightwear that feels wonderful to your skin and helps make you feel "pretty as a princess" in your own private world.

Touch is at the root of our deepest emotions.

COMFORTING BATHROOMS

Our bathrooms are overflowing with opportunities for touches of glorious comfort. Whether it be splashing cold water on our faces, sprinkling perfumed powder on our bodies, or snuggling into a soft, terry-cloth towel, our sense of touch can be greatly satisfied in this most private place of our homes. Next time you're in your bathroom preparing for the day or winding down the evening, think about ways that you can make the experience more pleasing to your tender touch. A few simple touches of convenient comfort can be very satisfying.

A Blissful Bath

Nothing is as soothing as slipping into a blissful bubbling bath. A good soak does wonders both physically and mentally. If you feel your life is about to take you over the edge, don't despair. Draw a hot bath for some rest, relaxation, and relief. The touch of water to your skin stimulates your circulation, calms your cluttered mind, relaxes your weary body, and soothes your tired muscles. Cool water revitalizes, lifting your spirits as you begin a new day. Warm water relaxes, calming your spirits as you wind down a busy day.

When the bathwater is running, add something extra for a spe-cial touch. A few drops of oil will silken your skin; a handful of oat-meal will soften the milky water; a splash of bubble bath will tickle you all over. The more convenient and comfortable your bathing experience, the more enjoyment it will bring. Keep all the necessary ingredients for a blissful bath nearby. Fill a pretty basket with favorite soaps, bubble bath, bath salts, lotions, sponges, and brushes. For another luxury, use a bath pillow to rest your head while soaking. Whether you like to read or just relax your neck and weary mind, this little touch will add comfort and joy to your time in the tub.

Drawing a warm bath for a loved one who you sense needs some tranquility is a wonderful act of love. Invite him or her to soak and relax in privacy. If you have young children, make bath time a fun time. Fill the tub with some colorful sponges and a few favorite plastic toys or cups. Watch them while they play — and clean themselves in the process! Wrap them in big plush towels, and give them lots of hugs and kisses. Then powder them all over with a fuzzy powder puff. When my niece and nephew visit, they often ask to take a bath in the middle of the day. Why? Because we make it a fun time of touch. The bath can truly be one life's simple pleasures.

"I can't think of any sorrow in the world that a hot bath wouldn't help, just a little bit."
— Susan Glaspell

A Stimulating Shower

Though the bathtub is a more relaxing form of cleaning our bodies, a stimulating shower can save time. We've all taken showers where just a drizzling stream of water sprouts from the shower head. It's an experience that is far from satisfying. For a revitalizing tingle, add an adjustable massage attachment to your showerhead. Adjust the massage control to pulsate the water pressure. The greater the water pressure, the more invigorating your shower will be.

Discover a soap that you love, not just for its fragrance, but for the feel of its shape in your hands and the texture of the lather it creates. One of life's little frustrations can be trying to lather your body with a crumbling bar of soap. Have a good supply of your favorite bar soaps on hand, and replenish your soap dish often. For lots of bubbles, lather liquid body soap on with a soft mesh buff. This is my favorite way to get clean and feel fresh while showering.

The Tickle of a Towel

When you finally step out of the bath or shower, have a soft, absorbent mat to dry your feet and prevent slipping. Pat yourself

dry with a thick terry cloth towel in a size and color that pleases you. Towels are available in a rainbow of colors and textures. Bath sheets as big as beach towels can wrap your whole body in warmth and comfort. Watch for midwinter white sales to replenish your towel supply. A fresh towel can bring a simple touch of satisfaction. If more than one person in your home is sharing the same bathroom, distinuguish towels by having different colors or monograms, or try stitching white towels with bands of different colored ribbons.

Treasure the gift of touch.

Several years ago, we were staying at a hotel for a marriage retreat. The accommodations were fairly nice, but the bath towels were not. They were so thin, I felt like I was drying my soaking body with a paper towel. It was certainly a touch the hotel had either overlooked or not made a priority. Unpleasant, as well as pleasant, touches can mark our memories.

Have a pretty towel bar or two to drape damp towels for drying. Wash towels frequently, and keep a good supply of fresh ones close at hand. Fill a large basket with rolled terry cloth towels or neatly stack bath towels on a dainty chair, stool, or wicker table. One of my favorite items in our bathroom is a big, forest green basket I stumbled across in a gift boutique. The sturdy wicker basket is lined and bowed with a beautiful floral fabric and is filled with rolls of our crisp, white, waffle-weave towels and washcloths. Anytime I reach for one, I feel pleasure.

For a real splurge, treat yourself to a towel-warming rack. The most luxurious hotels have them. A warming rack makes towels feel as though they are fresh from the dryer. A client friend of mine, Daughtry King, has a brass towel-warming rack given to her and her husband by their grown children. How thoughtful and generous! The rack now adorns their beautiful master bathroom, where they enjoy the warm touch it brings them every day.

Extra Touches

After you dry yourself off from the shower, complete the cleaning ritual by rubbing a favorite lotion all over your body to soothe and freshen your skin. Display the lotion in a decorative squirt dispenser or store it out of sight when not in use. Treasure the time you spend moisturizing your body; after all, it is God's temple — you need to care for it. Not only do I love the feel of my body lotion, I also enjoy the way it deeply moisturizes my body's skin and gives me a healthy glow.

For a terrific touch, cover your body with a fragrant dusting powder. The feel of a fluffy powder puff against your clean skin will make you feel like a new person! Store cotton swabs and soft cotton balls in pretty, glass decorative canisters on a bathroom shelf. They'll be close at hand for when you need a tiny touch to clean your body. For a colorful touch, try pastel cotton swabs and balls that coordinate with your bathroom decor.

Another way to care for your earthly body is to maintain proper body weight. Although I find weighing yourself every day a bit obsessive, it is a good idea to monitor your weight every now and then to prevent it from creeping out of control. Keep an accurate scale in your bathroom, and be sure to place it on a sturdy, solid surface when weighing yourself.

Recently, we were in the market for a new scale. I went to the store and was overwhelmed by the choices. I bought one of the least expensive ones thinking it didn't really matter as long as it weighed. When I brought it home, Bill and I each stepped on the scale several times. Every time we did, it showed each of us had lost another pound! For some, this may sound like the ideal scale, but it was certainly not helpful as an accurate monitor of our body weight. Needless to say, the scale was returned and upgraded to one that would do the job right. Don't sacrifice quality for price when purchasing a scale.

" . . . a time to embrace and a time to refrain . . ."
— Ecclesiastes 3:5

Whether you need a warm wrap after a shower or bath or a quick cover-up for your nightwear, have a comfortable bathrobe that's pleasing to your touch. Try a plush terry cloth or cozy chenille bathrobe. Crisp white is always a good color, or select a color that looks pretty in your home. Store your bathrobe on a big hook behind your bathroom door.

Because we wash our hands so many times during the day, make the experience as pleasant as possible. Keep a decorative dispenser of liquid soap by the sink for frequent handwashing. This simple habit can help keep your household healthy by preventing the spread of germs which lead to sickness. Fold or roll several small terry-cloth hand towels or washcloths in a basket by the sink for drying your hands or face.

Stock your bathroom with the necessary supplies to aid injuries and soothe aches and pains. Keep a heating pad, ice pack, soothing ointment, and first aid supplies. Try a foot massager to soak tired toes. Take the time to use your hands to bring comfort and loads of love to a family member who is sore or simply weary by giving a gentle rub to an aching limb, neck, or back. A small drop of baby oil will help your hands glide over their tired muscles. I have a dear friend whose husband loves for her to talk on the phone at night — the longer the better. Why? Because the whole time she chats, she gives him a massage.

"... if his hands are idle, the house leaks."
— Ecclesiastes 10:18

Comfortable Commodes

For a touch of convenience, keep several rolls of toilet paper that are pleasing to the touch stored underneath every bathroom sink. If cabinet space is limited, drop a few rolls in a small basket and place the basket beside the toilet.

Though we all dread it, the job of cleaning the bathroom must be done. I once heard a gifted Bible teacher say, "If Jesus Christ could labor all day in a carpenter's shop making tables, surely we can scrub a toilet now and then." As long as it has to be done, why not make the task of cleaning the bathroom as pleasant as possible? Store bathroom cleaning supplies underneath your sink for a quick cleanup.

Tiny Thought

Lord,
In my own home,
Where to do there is much,
May I slow myself down
And take time for touch.

Tips for a Touch of Comfort

Welcome with wonderful touches. Help overnight visitors feel at home with little touches of comfort like fresh towels, a bed of pretty linens, lots of plump pillows, and a cozy blanket or quilt.

Switch it. Use the small switch on your fan's axis to turn blades clockwise to stay cool in warm weather and counterclockwise to circulate heat in cold weather.

Open up. Bring the wonderful feel of the outdoors inside by opening your windows on a pleasant day and enjoying the fresh, soothing breeze as it flows through your home and touches your skin.

Keep it cozy. Use a tea cozy or tea towel around your teapot to keep your beverage warm. Transfer freshly brewed coffee to an airtight thermal carafe to keep it hot for several hours.

Get a grip. Transform a door or cabinet by replacing its hardware with beautiful, functional knobs or handles that feel wonderful to your grasp.

Watch the temperature. Place an outdoor thermometer outside your bedroom window. Check it in the morning as you dress for the day.

Hold on. A hold is a hug that hangs on. Sometimes a warm embrace provides more help and healing than any wise advise or wonder drug. Try to sense when the situation calls for you to zip your lip and reach out your arms to hold a loved one.

Touch a heart. For a touch of thoughtfulness, occasionally leave little sticky notes around your home for those you love. Put them where they're sure to be discovered — a mirror, phone receiver or a bed pillow.

Save it for a rainy day. For an effortless way to save toward something special for your home, keep a pretty jar on your bedroom dresser to store loose change from your purse or pockets.

Chapter Seven

~

The Heart of
the Home

*Above all else, guard your heart, for it is
the wellspring of life.*
Proverbs 4:23

THE HEART OF THE HOME

In the preceding sections, we have discussed the importance of filling our homes with pleasing sights, smells, tastes, sounds, and touches. Though each of these senses when stimulated can greatly affect the atmosphere of our homes, nothing has a more powerful influence on our surroundings than the attitude of our hearts. The kitchen is often referred to as the heart of the home, yet to me, the heart of the *homemaker* is the true heart of the home. A warm, loving home grows out of a warm, loving heart.

When it comes to creating a "SenseSational" home, Proverbs 4:23 offers some wise advice: "Above all else, guard your heart, for it is the wellspring of life." A wellspring is the fountain or source from which all other things flow. What we fill our hearts with, we will eventually fill our homes with. A miserable woman makes a miserable home. A joyful woman makes a joyful home. God has given us the incredible ability, as women, to set the atmosphere of our surroundings, for better or worse. The words and actions that set the atmosphere of our homes are simply an overflow of what we have stored up in our hearts.

"The best and most beautiful things in the world cannot be seen or touched but are felt in the heart."
— Helen Keller

A Healthy Heart

As wonderful as our senses are, we could survive without any one of them. There are many people who are blind, deaf, or mute who, despite their sensory loss, live healthy lives. There are those who suffer from chronic illnesses that cause temporary or permanent loss of smell and taste. Though they miss out on the pleasure these senses bring, they can still function. There are others, who from birth or an accident, have missing or paralyzed limbs. Though unable to touch and feel in these areas, they carry on.

The senses certainly enhance life, but they do not sustain it. The heart sustains life. God designed our heart to be the core of our being; it is essential to our earthly existence. The heart pumps the lifeblood to all parts of our body, so that each might function as God designed. When a heart is not healthy, it affects the whole body. Without a healthy heart, pursuing pleasant sights, sounds, smells, tastes, and touches is a pointless endeavor. Just as a physically healthy heart is vital for our bodies to function properly, a spiritually healthy heart is vital for our homes to function properly.

"The eye never has enough of seeing, nor the ear its fill of hearing."
— Ecclesiastes 1:8

A Heart for Christ

God created our senses to satisfy us, but only temporarily. We eat a delicious meal and are full and satisfied, yet hours later we are hungry again. We hear a beautiful song and our heavy hearts are uplifted, but later we return to discouragement. We smell a delightful fragrance, yet within minutes it is gone.

Though our senses can bring great pleasure to our lives, God never intended for them to satisfy us fully or to meet our greatest need. He alone can meet our most important need. The most beautiful castle filled with the richest foods and finest music could never come close to satisfying our primary need for a relationship with God.

In the book of Ecclesiastes, Solomon, the wisest man in the world, reflects on the purpose of life. After realizing that much in life can seem meaningless, Solomon states, "A man can do nothing better than to eat and drink and find satisfaction in his work" (Ecclesiastes 2:24a). But Solomon does not end there. He goes on to acknowledge that these pleasures are " . . . from the hand of God, for without him, who can eat or find enjoyment?" (Ecclesiastes 2:24b–25). Solomon's advice? There's more to life than just seeking pleasure; we must first seek God. Problems occur when we get so caught up in trying to be fulfilled by all the wonderful things life has to offer that we forget that God is the giver of all gifts. We begin to seek the blessing, not the blesser, the creation, not the creator, and then wonder why we are not satisfied.

A relationship with God through Jesus Christ is the only way to be fully satisfied forever. Jesus tells us in John 6:35, "I am the bread of life. He who comes to me will never go hungry, and he who believes in me will never be thirsty." Just as we need to awaken the senses in order to receive the blessings they can bring to life, so we need to awaken the heart to its need for Christ in order to enjoy the fullness of life that God intended. The greatest thing that you can do to make your home "SenseSational" is to allow Christ to dwell in your heart and take control of your life. Only with Christ in your life can your home truly reflect the joy and completeness of a satisfied heart.

Scripture tells us, "Unless the LORD builds the house, its builders labor in vain" (Psalm 127:1). The Lord is to be the heart, the centerpiece, the foundation of the home, and the principles found in his Word are to be the building blocks with which a strong and healthy home is built.

To me, making the Lord the heart of my home means building my home with the wisdom and knowledge of his Word. It means letting the fruit of his spirit — love, joy, peace, patience, kindness, goodness, faithfulness, gentleness, and self-control fill me and, in turn, fill my home. It means keeping a check on my priorities, remembering that relationships last and things do not. It means allowing God to be intricately involved in the details of my home life, trusting him to provide for my needs. And finally, it means keeping the proper perspective that my earthly home is only a temporary shelter, that my eternal home is the finest, final destiny.

"And my God will meet all your needs according to his glorious riches in Christ Jesus."
— Philippians 4:19

A Contented Heart

When it comes to your home, would you say that you have a contented heart? A contented heart is satisfied. To have a contented heart doesn't mean you don't still have hopes and dreams for what you'd like your home to be someday, but it does mean that your heart is filled with a quiet, gentle assurance that your life and your home are in God's loving hands. Are you grateful for where God has placed you? Are you blooming where he has planted you?

So often, we put our happiness on hold in hopes of a particular wish coming true. Perhaps you have grand illusions of a dream house with a white picket fence and a flower garden, but the home in which you now live is far from your dreams. Maybe you're longing for new living room furniture before you'll be satisfied. Perhaps you're waiting for your children to get older before bringing beauty and pleasure to your home. Today is the day that God has made — it is just as important as tomorrow. In fact, what we do in our homes

today may affect our attitude about tomorrow! What are you doing to make the most of your home life today?

Scripture tells us that where our treasure is our hearts will be as well. If your treasure in life is simply to satisfy yourself, then your home may be filled with lovely things, but your heart will still be empty. If, however, your treasure in life is Christ, and your goal is to seek him, then you will see your life and home as God's provisions and be grateful for them. You will be able to hold them with open hands, knowing that his plan for you can be trusted and is far greater than anything you could dream for yourself.

As an interior designer, I have had an opportunity to enter hundreds of homes and get an up close look at life behind the curtain. It is never as it seems. It's a lie to believe that as soon as you have a bigger home, a gourmet kitchen, a lovelier sofa, more money, a husband, children, or whatever your heart is longing for, you will be satisfied.

Have you put on hold the happiness your home can bring to you and those you love? What are you doing with the home God has given you? Is it a place of ministry or a place of misery? Allow God to minister to you as you minister to others through your home.

Your "SenseSational" Home

The outward beauty of a home can be captivating, but the inner beauty of a heart has far more potential to bless others. The fragrances we fill our homes with can be delightful, but the sweet aroma of Christ is the longest-lasting fragrance we can release. The soothing music we fill our homes with will certainly please the ears, but loving words from a Christ-filled heart can soothe the soul. The wonderful touch of furnishings may bring comfort, but they cannot begin to compare to the joy of a life that has been touched with the love of God. Delicious foods may temporarily meet our physical needs, but Jesus Christ is the only one that can feed our spirits and satisfy us fully.

While you strive to awaken the senses to bring life and love to your home, remember that the condition of your heart will be the most influential ingredient in setting the atmosphere. After all, the heart of the homemaker is the heart of the home. May Christ bless your home with life and love as he inhabits your heart.

"Godliness with contentment is great gain."
— 1 Timothy 6:6

"The house of the righteous contains great treasure ..."
— Proverbs 15:6

Tiny Thought

Lord,
If there could be a blessing
To others I'd impart,
May it be that I filled my home
With a contented, Christ-filled heart.

ACKNOWLEDGMENTS

As my hand comes to the close of writing this book, my mind is flooded with memories of all that has transpired, and my heart is filled with love and gratitude towards all who have made these pages possible.

Proverbs 15:22 states, "Plans fail for lack of counsel, but with many advisors they succeed." Indeed, this book's development has had many advisors, and each has contributed significantly in his or her own way to its final outcome. Thank you, thank you, thank you . . .

First and foremost, thank you to my Heavenly Father, who clearly led me to write this book and faithfully guided my thoughts and my pen. You alone are to be glorified for any blessing this book may bring.

To my precious husband, Bill — Thank you for believing in what God could do through me, when I did not. I love you, honey! Thanks for encouraging me to go away to write so I could focus on what God called me to do; and then when I returned, the endless hours of sitting by my side at the computer reviewing the manuscript. You balance me, guide me, and help me keep things in perspective. I love sharing life and our home together. You are my greatest gift from God!

To my parents — I'm sure you never dreamed the little investments you made into my life and our home would ever be shared in a book. Neither did I! Thank you for loving me by making our house a warm and welcoming home. Your sacrifices, support, and continual prayers have blessed me beyond words. May your legacy bring you honor.

To John Trent and Tim Kimmel — You guys are incredible! Thanks for paving the publishing way and encouraging me to write this book. God used you both to direct my steps. Your awesome writings have richly blessed so many. Thanks for your friendships and your investment.

To Mike Hyatt and Robert Wolgemuth — Who would have thought when we met three years ago that this book would ever finally be born? Thank you Mike and Robert, for listening to my passion for the home, catching the vision and running with it. Your counsel and expertise have been invaluable.

To Sandy VanderZicht and Joy Marple — Two years ago, you flew to Atlanta to visit me right after we had moved into our home, and you *still* wanted me to write this book! You truly believed in this project by faith and not by sight! I am extremely grateful for your willingness to publish my heartbeat for the home. It has been a joy to work with you both.

To Scott Bolinder — Thank you for believing in this project before we ever met face-to-face. Your enthusiasm for this book's message has encouraged me greatly, and I am thankful to serve our Lord with the Zondervan team.

To Rachel Boers — What a blessing you have been as my editor! The minute we met, I knew we'd click. Thank you for your investment in this project. Your hard work and wise insights have clarified and helped to communicate the message of this book. You're the best!

To Edsel Arnold — God has gifted you greatly with your hands, my friend, and he blessed me greatly when you agreed to work on this project. You've made this book beautiful with your talented touch. Thank you for your patience and perseverance. May the fruit of your labor be rich and satisfying!

To all the design crew — Sherri Hoffman, Jody Langley, Robin O'Brien, and Anne Huizinga — Thank you for putting up with designing a book for a designer! You have been wonderful, and I appreciate your hard work and partnership on this project.

To all my special friends and family members who have prayed for me — Your prayers and encouragement have sustained me. Thank you for loving me.

Lastly, thanks go out to you, the reader, for reading this book. I pray God uses it to bless your home and all those who enter it. You are loved!

terry

If you liked *Creating a SenseSational Home*, you'll love Terry Willits' five small (5 1/2 x 6 1/2) hardcover books, one on each of the senses.

These books of practical tips offer simple and affordable ways to make your home an environment of beautiful looks, soothing sounds, fragrant smells, comforting touches, and tantalizing tastes. Inspiring and beautifully illustrated with two-color line drawings, these are books you'll want to keep within easy reach. Great for gift-giving at showers and house warmings.

101 Quick Tips to Make Your Home Feel SenseSational, 0-310-20228-0, $9.99
101 Quick Tips to Make Your Home Feel SenseSational helps you add fresh dimensions of comfort to your home through the resourceful use of touch and texture.

101 Quick Tips to Make Your Home Look SenseSational, 0-310-20224-8, $9.99
101 Quick Tips to Make Your Home Look SenseSational will open your eyes to the beauty already in your home and inspire you with fresh ideas for added touches of color, elegance, and warmth.

101 Quick Tips to Make Your Home Smell SenseSational, 0-310-20225-6, $9.99
101 Quick Tips to Make Your Home Smell SenseSational offers simple and inspiring ideas for enhancing the atmosphere of your home through the tasteful use of flowers, sachets, scented lamp rings, and the smell of freshly baked bread.

101 Quick Tips to Make Your Home Sound SenseSational, 0-310-20227-2, $9.99
101 Quick Tips to Make Your Home Sound SenseSational will convince you of the importance of what fills your ears—and what doesn't fill them—in making your home a place of peace and spiritual and emotional refreshment.

101 Quick Tips to Make Your Home Taste SenseSational, 0-310-20226-4, $9.99
101 Quick Tips to Make Your Home Taste SenseSational offers common-sense and innovative ideas for enticing the tastebuds with healthy, delicious food and beverages, keeping in mind that the most pleasing foods are often the simplest.

SenseSational Home Daybreak™ Perpetual Calendar, 0-310-96330-3, $9.99
366 quick tips and ideas for making your home a place that fills the senses and nourishes the spirit every day of the year.

Terry Willits' books and calendar are available at fine bookstores everywhere.

ZondervanPublishingHouse
Grand Rapids, Michigan
http://www.zondervan.com

A Division of HarperCollinsPublishers

America Online
AOL Keyword:zon